Piece by Piece

Remembering Georgina:
A Mother's Memoir

HELEN VICTORIA ANDERSON

Slipway Press

Praise for *Piece by Piece*

Piece by Piece is extraordinarily moving and beautifully written - there is such powerful attention to detail here that the reader is given new insight into grief and love. This memoir is a testament to Helen Anderson's strength and courage - her honesty is unflinching: *Piece by Piece* demands to be read by everyone.

- Marion Husband, author of *The Boy I Love* trilogy, *The Good Father, Say You Love Me*, and *Six Little Deaths*

To say *Piece by Piece* is a moving memoir wouldn't do justice to the raw honesty on every page. I cried so many times as I read Helen's story of losing her lovely Georgina so young and trying to cope with the pain and sorrow that are with her day in, day out. Helen is a wonderful, heartfelt, descriptive writer and her grief is tangible, yet she is not only surviving every mother's worst nightmare, she is chronicling it as a life lesson for the rest of us. She is one brave lady to let us into a heart that has been through so much.

- Christine Fieldhouse, author of *Why Do Monsters Come Out at Night?*

Piece by Piece is more than a compelling story of death and grief. It is a story of love: the love of strangers; the love of the community and the love of an amazing family.

- Karen Charlton, author of *The Detective Lavender Mysteries*

As a mother who has also lost a child to cancer, I completely identify with the range of emotions which are perfectly encapsulated in Helen's memoir. The overwhelming sense of loss and longing for your child, of no longer knowing your purpose, and of trying to find a way through the pain to discover a new life which is acceptable enough for you to want to learn to live again... These are real quandaries in the tragedy of child-loss, and I believe that this book will help many people realise they are not alone, others have walked this path before, and that somehow, they too will survive.

- Leona Knox, mother of wee Oscar

FOR MY CHILDREN, WITH LOVE

FOREWORD

At the beginning of July 2013, I was trying to 'make it' as a writer. I had recently won first prize in a national short story competition. My son, Joe, had just finished his second year at university. My husband, Paul, and I lived in the sleepy North-East town of Marske-by-the-Sea with our fourteen year-old daughter, Georgina, who was also trying to 'make it' – but as a singer. We were looking forward to taking Georgina and her friend, Amber, on holiday to France, as soon as school broke up for summer. We were moving forward with our lives.

Georgina had struck me as slightly pale, but it was hard to tell, because she was experimenting with fake tan. For a few weeks, she had felt a burning under her ribs which was not touched by the antacid suggested by our GP. I hauled her back to the doctor. He said it might be gallstones, but that she was really too young for them. An out-of-hours trip to A&E as Georgina writhed in pain resulted in the recommendation of a non-urgent ultrasound. Paul set about badgering our local hospital for any cancellations, so that this whole thing could be sorted out and we could tell our travel insurers what was what.

On Monday 15th July, a last-minute slot came up, and our daughter's abdomen was scanned. Hours later, a different GP from our practice phoned with news of a 'mass' on my daughter's liver. Her voice was grim, in spite of her attempts to reassure. We were to take Georgina back to the hospital the next morning. There, to our increasing alarm, we were redirected fifty miles away, to the regional children's oncology unit.

On Thursday 18th July 2013, a team of doctors gathered around Georgina's hospital bed and delivered the news that she had a cancerous tumour on her liver. Stage Four. There isn't another stage after Stage Four: I know, because my fierce daughter asked outright. She demanded the truth. And the truth was that it had already spread to her lungs. The situation was now deemed urgent. Serious. But there were known instances of successfully tackling similar cancers. There was still some hope.

Piece by Piece is a transcript of the journal that I began to keep, from that day. It started out as therapy. My notebook was somewhere to pour all my fears and crazy thoughts, as I tried to look like I was holding things together. Rather than trying to detail the course of Georgina's illness and treatment, I used the pages of my journal to impose some order on the chaos around and inside of me. I began to record my psychological journey as the parent of a teenager with cancer - as a floundering new member of the 'club' that nobody ever asks to join.

Where there are gaps in my account, because I was too preoccupied or distressed to write, I have added social media posts and press excerpts from that period. Together with my later reflections about my daughter, these chart my response to the course of Georgina's illness and to the stunning, worldwide reaction to her music.

Piece by Piece is a memoir based on my perspective of events experienced during those months of crisis. It is not intended as a complete, factual record but as an honest, raw snapshot of turbulent times. It is also a testament to my daughter's courage and talent, as well as to the strength of our family, her friends and the wider community.

Several times, I have been approached by journalists who claim to want to tell Georgina's story. I have always replied that I cannot speak on Georgina's behalf. I do not have that right. But I do have my own story, as the mother of this amazing young woman. The words in *Piece by Piece* are mine, and mine alone, but I hope that they will resonate with anyone who has ever feared losing a loved one and that they may bring a little comfort, in some way, to others who find themselves facing the unthinkable.

- Helen Victoria Anderson. November 2015.

Biopsy day. They're taking chunks of her. Taking her away from me piece by piece. They're cutting out the badness, though there's not a bad cell in her body. Virgin, uncut skin. Outside, it is tropical. *Please do not open the windows. We operate a clean air policy for the sake of our teenagers and children.* I wait on the fold-down bed, with the holey mint green blanket crumpled beneath me. I wait for her to come out the other side. Knowing she'll soon be gone again.

My daughter wanted to keep her socks on, in theatre. They are pale-blue – lace-edged. Top Shop, or maybe Primark – it seems less important than a month ago. It's less important than it was last week, when she bought sundresses and hot-pants and flip-flops for kicking around in. When we still had the summer ahead of us, with the promise of theme parks and end-of-school parties in the back garden and of being chatted up by French boys around the campsite pool.

Someone has flicked the switch to winter in here. Winter without Christmas. Should I have spotted it earlier? Should I have kicked and screamed in the GP's surgery? Should I have blocked the door in A&E when they sent us back to the GP – back to square one? All the time, it was multiplying, until it was 5cm by 6cm (probably bigger today, even with the bits chopped out).

Bring her back to me – whole. I promise I don't care about not going to the Côte d'Azur. Just as long as she's okay. I need her to be okay. I fix my eyes on the ins-and-outs of the nurse's

1

fish-tail plait as we walk back to the ward to wait. Her rubberised shoes slip off her heels. She clip-clops and asks if I'm okay. Her accent suggests that she is far from home. She is almost a child herself, like my daughter.

"I need to toughen up", I say.

She doesn't know what to say.

I phone to tell my mother what is happening. I want my mother. I am the mother. I wait in the bedroom with the funky purple lights. I consider all the buttons on the panel. I could have a disco, if I wanted. Silent, because the radio in the bathroom's not working. I switch on the giant television opposite the state-of-the-art bed. *Made in Chelsea*. Irritating. But I will watch *Made in Chelsea* for the rest of my life, if that's what it takes to get Georgina better. Such are the bargains I'm making with God, Fate, The Universe, or Whoever.

Sunday, 21st July 2013.

We cobbled together a party yesterday afternoon. My husband Paul and I stuck chairs and loungers on the lawn and served pizzas and hot dogs and the young people came. They all wanted a selfie with Georgina and they were all brave. She has good friends.

Now she's upstairs in her bedroom. She strums the guitar softly, then more surely. She fears she has lost her singing voice but I'm sure I hear a whisper of it. I drove her to McDonalds for a Happy Meal. It works until sympathy-smiles sour her smoothie. Like the tumour on her liver branching out into her fourteen-year-old lungs, news has spread fast.

I sit at the table on our sun-baked patio and examine the back garden. My domain. The lawn is patched with golden straw, where the blades could no longer hold in the moisture. Their sap has been sucked out, evaporating into the furnace of the air. Ready to fall somewhere else, when the temperature drops. The weed-killer Paul applied last week – before all this started - has done its job. The dandelion leaves between the paving slabs are brown. Dandelion potpourri. You kid yourself that you can control them but they'll pop up again. We'd never garden at all, if we acknowledged what we're up against. We'd let it turn itself back wild and allow ivy creepers to reclaim our houses. Or we'd pave the whole lot over, or carpet it with fake turf and try to ignore the static shock. The table top looks like a wrought-iron treacle tart but it is odourless. Perhaps I have lost my sense of smell, along with my knees' ability to lock and take my weight.

The sunshine helps. I drink it in as if I'm storing up its life force. In a fit of pathetic fallacy, pewter clouds are gathering: storms forecast. The wind catches the tin foil windmills that I staked around the borders yesterday, to brighten the garden up for her gathering. I thought Georgina might think them unsophisticated, but she 'gets' that they are ironic. Kitsch. I leave them in their places. They can still turn, without the sun.

We drive up to Tesco, trying to find titbits to tempt her to eat. Hot chocolate. Princess marshmallows. Long life milk. These are the days of normality before the chaos starts. Already, we are arranging ourselves into unexpected patterns. Ready to splinter off. Floating back together again. These are the most unusual days of my life. Will I look back and say "This was a happy time"? I hope the long life milk does what it says on the carton.

Tomorrow, we will go back to the hospital to hear the doctors' plan. I hope that there is one. I count the vases of flowers in our lounge. Ten. I didn't know we had ten vases. Orange lilies. Yellow lilies. Pink lilies. They might not even be lilies at all. I don't know the names of all these flowers. I don't have the words. There is no language for all of this. Chrysanthemums, maybe. Gerbera (I know the word for this but I can't pronounce it because I've never heard it spoken out loud). Roses (magenta). Cultivated, boxed, express-delivered.

Carnations. My mind flits to tinned peaches with condensed milk, in my grandma's kitchen. Shuddering jelly and crushed pineapple luxury. Tongue sandwiches. Trying to get my head around the idea that 'tongue' actually was a real animal's *tongue*. I think of Grandma's salads, in the days when 'salad' meant a lettuce and half a tomato and a hard-boiled egg with membrane slivers and shell fragments still attached. I remember the wobbly whiteness when the last of the casing was peeled off, ready for the salt to be poured on it. Ready for the bone-handled knife.

Tuesday, 23rd July 2013.

Helen Anderson posted:
Sneaking a 'glass' (*ahem) of wine before retiring ready for an early start tomorrow.

Wednesday, 24th July 2013.

Helen Anderson posted:
Georgina is back home until Monday, while they come up with a plan xx

Paul Anderson posted:
Update on Georgina Anderson. The hospital still isn't sure what type of cancer it is exactly. They're doing more analysis of the samples & sending them to London. They've said it is a very rare cancer which means they aren't quite sure how to treat it, but they are planning to with drug treatment. We'll be coming back in on Monday, to get a permanent line put in with a small operation, to hopefully start treatment next week xx

Friday, 26th July 2013.

Still just within an inch of formulating a plan. Plans can be slippery customers. There's no certainty to be found, anywhere. Certainty is a cognitive illusion.

Our elderly neighbour still pushes her shopping trolley to the village centre, for her daily rations. It keeps her busy, like polishing her letterbox. It gives her a chance to 'bump into' someone who might listen to her chatter. She tries to be subtle as she bustles past our house.

5

From my lookout point upstairs, I see her staring back, before she disappears into the alleyway further up the road. She thinks I can't see her, not looking. What does she expect to see, through our double-glazing?

Maybe it's time to get vertical blinds installed, even if they do remind me of the office. I haven't worked in an office for ten years, thank God, but never say "never". In half an hour, our neighbour's head will re-appear over the alley fence. She will trundle her trolley, slower, looking everywhere but at this house. But she won't cross over until the very last minute. She will choose her route carefully.

Words like 'chemo' and 'Hickman line' are starting to lurch from my tongue. They are not yet flying or tripping – I haven't grasped the finer points of this new language. I don't ever want to be fluent. I am just learning Conversational Cancer-Speak (non-accredited, flexible family-learning).

My daughter is finding her voice. It is not the same as before the news, but it is still hers. She is pinning it down onto tape. She is setting down tracks in case she loses herself and needs to find her way home. Her recordings are like a pebble path; a trail of cake crumbs is too easily pecked away. There are woodcutters in this dark forest. They may just be going about their business, completely benign. Or they may be assassins.

<u>Monday, 29th July 2013.</u>

The line is in. The way to Georgina's heart is via a hole next to her collar-bone. They haven't started delivering the poison but her insides are already turning themselves inside out.

This high-tech hospital room is lime green, with purple accents. Colour pop. Trendy. I wonder which shapes and fabrics we'll be wearing, a year from now. What will be the new season's black? Out of the window, we have a prime view of the university, devoid of students. They have graduated and gone. The first day, I saw them with their parents and their step-parents, launching into the world, with their certificates in hand.

Blue signs with white letters point to the city's heart. We are watching *X-Factor*. *X-Factor* re-runs, to be precise: *The Best and Worst of X-Factor*. This is The Worst of Times. I am not really watching. On the ivory tower opposite is a wrought-iron weather vane. I work out my bearings, via its North and South. I am told I am west. I look down on the hospital car park. *No Exit. Drop Off Only. One Way.*

<u>Wednesday, 31st July 2013.</u>

Now, my daughter looks ill. She has the essential accessories like the bile-filled gastro-nasal tube taped to her cheek. We pull her skinny legs into white anti-DVT stockings and try to smooth out the wrinkles at the knees, like I used to with her ballet tights when she was a dot. She sports a surgical gown, rather than a pink leotard and net tutu. I remember how she never had patience with 'barre' (i.e. chair back) work: she was always too eager for the part where they could 'interpret' the music, free of choreography, and sprinkle fairy dust with her plastic glitter wand.

All those years of afternoons spent anxiously waiting in the cloakroom with the other mothers for the quick-change into black, shiny tap shoes. The racket of her toes testing their click on the community centre parquet. The clacking of steel drip stands on hospital lino. All that effort to manoeuvre herself to partner up with the most popular girl, as the mothers grabbed seats around the edge of the end-of-term session – a special treat to be allowed in to witness our daughters' progress, in person, rather than pressing our noses up to the glass door. A special treat not to have to view their tiny pink forms through the chicken-wire supporting the pane from the inside, like a bird's skeleton.

Thursday, 1st August 2013.

These are my 'morning pages', which every writer's supposed to use to empty their minds of the night's thoughts and feelings, before the real business of creating stories begins. Ideally, every day. Yeah, right. But I am writing this morning, because writing is what has kept me sane-ish for the last two years. If I need anything, right now – apart from for Georgina to live - it is to remain sane.

I am growing used to the beeping machines which feed the precious poisons into her but I stay alert to the retching and heaving and the stomach storms which signal the urgency to unhook her and trundle to the en-suite. This two metre stretch from bed to bathroom is long.

I feel as if I'm trying to learn to swim and my legs don't even feel like they'll make it halfway across. And everyone else is sailing lengthwise, criss-crossing our path and drowning us with their perfect technique. It's as if an evil swimming instructor has made me set off, knowing fine well that I can't reach the bottom unless I submerge my head. I have tried doggy paddle and treading water, but I'm at the stage of wondering why I have to learn at all. Surely, I could just stay away from water for the rest of my life?

But there's water, water everywhere. Danger. I am sinking to the base of a submerged quarry, like a chunk of stone hewn from its own sides. Chlorine shoots up my nose, catching my throat, like that tube siphoning green-black sediment from my daughter's stomach-bed. Our eyes sting from the noxious chemicals added specifically to save our bodies from being invaded.

Friday, 2nd August 2013.

At her bedside. Her tiny fist curls around my forefinger like a newborn's. I marvel at her pale half-moons. I follow the course of the grey-blue veins through her translucent wrists. I resist the urge to prod each dimple on her knuckles.

My daughter wakes and her eyes meet mine. Her eyes rest on me for a good while. A mother learns to take this weight. My daughter speaks:

"I'm bored".

I paint her long finger nails candy-floss pink. I apply a second coat, because we have time. On each ring finger, I add an accent of peppermint, as we have seen in her magazines. Top-coat, now, but I know that those half-moons are still under there. She holds her hands out at arm's length and half smiles. She is allowing herself to feel happy with this unweakened part of this body of hers.

Saturday, 3rd August 2013.

You can tell that it's the weekend, because there's a sole junior doctor haunting the hospital corridors. Do brand new, shiny wings of buildings have ghosts, if they are built on the site of old ones? This atrium connects the glass and steel of the children's hospital to the brick and tiles of the old infirmary. It is all connected. You can see the joins.

If ghosts can walk through walls, why aren't they everywhere? Why do they stay trapped in a single haunted house?

Tuesday, 6th August 2013.

I am a bad mother. I know this. I know this because I failed to wake when my daughter needed me, during the night. She needed to expel some of those extra fluids they're pumping into her. She had to unplug herself and wrestle with the drip stand. She dragged herself across those interminable two metres and opened the bathroom door right next to where I was lying on my fold-up bed. I did not wake.

I thought it was all part of my nightmare, where my child was being taken away from me, for taking smack. I was finding out in my dreams that the dream baby in my dream stomach had stopped moving. That the baby was a tumour. That the baby never really existed at all. In all of this nightmare, I missed my real child's cry of "Mammy". She never calls me that any more.

We have been introduced to more professionals. Like the team we have already met, they are nice enough. Exceptionally smiley, in fact. I am dangerously close to crying, when people are kind to me. I focus on keeping my cool. On holding it together, retaining my equilibrium, and all the other phrases which sound simple enough. I am handed business cards and welcomed to a place I don't want to be. There are explanations of roles I didn't know existed.

"Any questions?"

I have none: I think we've covered everything, except 'Why?'

Saturday, 10th August 2013.

I open the page of this notebook, which Georgina bought me for Mother's Day, and a strand of hair falls onto the duvet. It is long and brown – lightened at the tip. Dip-dyed. I insisted she had it done properly at a hairdressers, if she really had to do it. It has a forked ending. I separate the split end and peel one side down. It splits again, over and over, like a cancerous cell multiplying its mistakes. Tomorrow, more hairs will be shed, as the poison works its magic on her follicles – this poison which we have signed for, consenting to its attack on her teenage body. Over and over.

It is 10p.m. and The Sick Children's Trust has kindly given me accommodation right next to the hospital, while Paul stays with our daughter. There's only room for one of us. It's a well-kept, calm place, inhabited by frantic parents of desperately ill children. I cast my eyes down, when I pass other families in the hallway, unable to take on any more pain. We are over the road from A&E on a Saturday night. I fear that there will be no peace for me, tonight.

This charity does an excellent job and the room does its best, with its Scandi shabby-chic whites and creams. I am caught in blizzard of bad news – a total whiteout. I am looking forward to a night of blankness, without the bleeps and beeps. Without the hourly puffing of the blood pressure cuff and my daughter's croaky thanks to the nurses. Such good manners, in spite of her bad mother.

I listen to the sirens; the car engines; the sing-song voices. A baby cries for its sick sibling in the next room. The taps in the shared bathroom on the landing groan. I am pleased, for all our sakes, to note that the radiators are coated with anti-bacterial paint. A laminated notice on the bedroom door gently suggests ways to raise funds to help. I feel as if I am laminated, too. Feeling the pain, but not quite, like through a condom or their blue examination gloves. I don't know who the extra layer's meant to be protecting.

I am told that the dog is adjusting well to staying with his grandad and to his rota of walkers. I don't know why this comes to mind. I imagine him stopping and sniffing the ground, whenever and wherever the fancy takes him. If I could feel anything, I would be glad for him.

<u>Sunday, 11th August 2013.</u>

It is morning. I shower and dress. It's important to maintain some kind of standards, in the interests of holding myself together, so I blow-dry and straighten my hair. I wait for the straighteners to cool down so that I can pack them in my rucksack and head back to Georgina. I scrub my name out on the whiteboard in the entrance, so they don't look for me if there's a fire. Outside A&E, I pause at the drop-off point to absorb the rays bouncing off the tarmac. Then I head past the hungover relics of last night's festivities.

Sunday mornings are the worst time, when they all come to, and notice that they're in pain. Turn left past Minor Injuries and into the corridor which leads to the corridor where a sign dangles on steel chains from the ceiling. As usual, I gulp with surprise, as I take in the black letters - stark, like bald heads on their shiny white background. *Teenage Cancer Unit.*

<u>Monday, 12th August 2013.</u>

Coffee. I long for bitter, hot coffee, edged with foam. I would sip it from a white china bowl, flawless from the kiln. I want to swish it around my gums and push it through the gaps in my teeth, feeling the grounds left behind when the liquid has been swallowed. I want to sit in the Place du Commerce in Nantes and watch ladies with chignons and classic white shirts kiss each other hello on both cheeks and drink from teeny-tiny dolls' cups and kiss each other goodbye on both cheeks before they wander among the hens strung up in the market. Already dead. Still wriggling.

I long for other things.

Tuesday, 13th August 2013.

I was going to leave a blank page between each entry. I was going to separate each day, but they're all running into one. Then, it occurred to me that this paper might be all I've got and I should make the most of every single scrap. I plan to fill it, with no space for afterthoughts or corrections.

The patients' parents swap stories and bravado in the ward kitchen, but I try to heat my meals when it is empty. They say that a problem shared is a problem halved, and it is tempting to offload. But I don't want to transfer a portion of my despair to people whose plates are already spilling over. By day, we wear a uniform of easy-wash non-iron, clothes. I have three outfits with me, which I wear in rotation. At night, we parents wear pyjamas, which must be modest, in case we need to roam from our child's room to fetch sick bowls or deliver bed pans to the sluice. I wear a multi-stretch bra under my nightclothes. Standards. Somehow, these things seem to matter.

My daughter is asleep. Last night, we talked about sorting her childhood photos into albums.

"Then they'll be ready for my funeral". She held my gaze.

"Don't say things like that." I could manage nothing better, in response. Nothing more hopeful. Nothing more convincing. I don't believe in making false promises, but I wish I did.

Now, I don't want to put any photos in any albums. Now, I want to leave all our pictures of the past higgledy-piggledy in their boxes and wallets, along with the birthday cards and the nursery school artwork which showed such promise. Along with the lock of her fuzzy first head of hair, I want to bundle them back in the loft and let the dust settle back on them. I never want to have a reason to get them down and to look back.

I have been trained in using mindfulness to get through times of crisis, so I focus on the hospital décor. I describe it to myself. I am writing it down, to stop myself from talking out loud, which is not the 'done thing':

The walls are decorated in funky lime. The clock provides a touch of funky purple. The roller blinds pull down to reveal a giant psychedelic barcode. But still, the blankets on the bed are a washed out, hospital shade of mint. Not going with anything. Not exactly clashing with anything. An institutional mint, lest we wake and momentarily think we're in a boutique hotel. Mint, like toothpaste, taking away the taste of anything delicious we might ever have savoured.

Thursday, 15th August 2013.

It is only just still Thursday. Still twenty minutes to go. Still twenty minutes until they take her temperature. This – the third reckoning in three hours – will be decisive. At stake are five days at home – five days of 'normal'. If having tubes protruding from your chest and being fed a cappuccino-coloured cocktail via your nose is 'normal'.

I've learned to fill her tube and set the machine to keep on topping her up throughout the night. I've yet to summon the courage to stick a needle in her slim thigh, but her dad obliges. I am glad of his strength. I have the pack of gauze and tape and spare ports and clamps and sterile wipes in my non-sterile, bulging handbag. We thought we were ready for these semi-promised five days. Now, once more, it is a case of waiting and seeing.

I wonder if the lack of news about her brain scan is ominous. Don't they say "no news is good news"? Or is no news simply postponed bad news, waiting for a consultant to deliver it in a cool, quiet interview room? Quiet, except for the roar of the air purifier. My menopausal skin registers the chill. I break out in terrible goose bumps while we skirt around the giant elephant in the room. Avoiding that conversation which has already been played out, every which way, at the back of my mind; at the front and sides of my mind; in the very deepest and darkest corners. The great grey beast cowers in the corners, not daring to show itself. Whimpering and hissing like the vital clean air system.

Thursday, 22nd August 2013.

Been home. My fourteen-year-old shaved off the remains of her hair. Her friend, Chloe, has shaved hers, too, to make her feel better and I came home to their giggle fits.

"My hair's in the bath, Mum".

I fished it out and wrapped it in newspaper. I threw it in the outside bin like a bird mauled by a moggy, with the feeling that I should have given it a more dignified despatch – a fitting send-off. That hair was much-loved and it has served her well. But her features more than cope without it and her scalp covers her skull snugly enough. I remember the weight of her newborn head. The constant reminders to support her neck. I remember the fear of dropping something important. The fear of forgetting something. I fear remembering.

We are back in hospital again, but when I was at home, I managed to write my blog. People said it was brave and beautiful. I feel scared, not brave. Yet not exactly cowardly, either. Is there a better word for someone who's trying to be brave but still perfecting the art? Not quite achieving bravery but putting their all into its pursuit?

Friday, 23rd August 2013.

This room in the charity accommodation – for which I am unspeakably grateful – reminds me of a hall of residence. Of a hostel. Of a halfway house. I am halfway to hope and halfway to the place nobody wants to go.

I focus on this new room. There are five notices on the door. There is a sink in a vanity unit backed with lemon tiles exactly like the ones my parents ripped out in the 1980s. There are hospital-fabric curtains. A pattern of blue, lemon, mint, terracotta - abstract with a hint of the waves of a sea and the flow of a river from one patch to another. Triangles suggest a yacht, now that I have gone down this mental route. A solid green rectangle with yellow squares becomes a fisherman's hut with sun glowing through open windows. I feel the air blowing through. Or it may all be totally abstract. Patterns of nothingness, repeated. I make out a Maldives beach hut on stilts – paradise sinking, before I have even been to it.

Tuesday, 27th August 2013.

The mothers of sick children ought not to swear, but I am exploding with expletives, which I transcribe as plosives, sibilants and asterisks. In the corner of my daughter's sick room, I silently scribble about being criticised by her father. It feels as though my failings are the topic of the week. Over and over, they are highlighted and underlined by my husband, as we turn each other into substitutes for the real, unseen enemy. We battle, in full sight of the sick-bed, barrels nominally muted.

I am not a trained nurse. I am not a trained mother. I do the best I can in these circumstances into which I have been ditched. I can't remember the last time Paul said a nice word to me. I have been out of his field of vision for weeks, only

18

picked up as a potential threat. Any movement is a threat, in these waters. I feel as if he's sending in the big guns; U-boats. Torpedoes. Neutralise.

He says it's all in my imagination, but I feel he enjoys the crunch of me under his heel, as he grinds me into the lino, along with the glitter that the nurses sprinkle on discharged teenage boys, and the abandoned plastic thermometer cases. Like domestic waste. Clinical waste. One big waste.

Nobody's perfect, and perfection's not even something I strive for these days. I have learned that seeking perfection is a mug's game. A losing battle. A hiding to nothing. I know that you only chase perfection around and around until you're caught in a vortex and you don't know your bum from your gob. I won't go there again. It has nearly broken me, before. I won't even follow his chase with my gaze. It makes me dizzy. Sick.

I am not the enemy here, but friendly fire still produces coffins. It sometimes feels like we are a family at war. I sign treaty after treaty, in the face of loss after loss. Day after day, my husband transforms his frustration with the situation into an aversion to me. It's as though we're in the middle of an acrimonious divorce and he's holding back killer insults purely for the child's sake. Day after day, he disguises his disgust with my failure to make this thing right, less carefully. I don't know if I can do this. I don't know.

Wednesday, 4th September 2013.

Back to school, for some. Back to hospital, for us. Georgina wants to be out again, as soon as possible, so she is willing her temperature down. She wants her freedom – freedom to go back to school, even if it will only be for two days, before we are back here for more drugs through drips. I daren't buy her new school uniform yet, because she is shrinking. She is shrinking out of her old clothes and growing back into her child-body.

We thought that our out-patient clinic trip would be a quick in-and-out job. We allowed ourselves to think we might have got away with it. Now, a few days at home are an achievement – a prize to be fought for. They were just within grasping distance. I could feel their solidity and their cool, silver contours. I could almost taste them, but they've been locked back in the cabinet, out of reach. I press my nose to the glass, but I can't smell anything. The light catches the trophy differently. It is there, but lacklustre. I can see that it is silver plate, wearing thin, to show the plastic underneath, like the replica World Cup my dad bought for my brother in 1966.

I wanted that cup. I wanted my dad to have bought it for me, even if I was two years off being even a twinkle in his eye, then. It made no pretence of being real, but I marvelled at the mock-veined, mock-marble base and the seams on the handles where the two halves of the mould had been fixed together. Victory, slightly dusty.

My brother sometimes let me in his room. He had white textured vinyl on the walls, purple curtains and purple mottled carpet. He had a white PVC headboard screwed to a divan with bendy chipboard drawers. A noticeboard, with posters of Deep Purple and Black Sabbath and Blondie. Later, Kim Wilde, probably not for musical reasons.

It was definitely a teenager's bedroom, like the one we have been allocated this time, in the hospital. Purple walls, like my least favourite Tootie Frooties flavour.

In this shared bay, you can't control the temperature. The nurses make a centralised decision. They take everyone's needs into account. My hot flushes are not in the equation. I strip off to jeans and a vest top. There are only so many layers I can peel off before I am totally inappropriate.

Friday, 6th September 2013.

Helen Anderson posted:
G's temp has 'spiked' again (get me with my super-medical lingo!). Boooo. She had her heart set on going to Emily's birthday but it looks unlikely xx

Friday, 6th September 2013.

Killing time while Georgina watches yet another romcom, cuddled up with her dad in the hospital bed. She's falling out, so he curves his arm around her. Hairy bristle on soft, disappearing down. Each of her follicles is weakening, burning itself out as it races to renew itself. I am killing time, when I should be conserving it. I need to save this time forever.

21

I am killing time until she's ready for bed, proper, and needs me to help her shed her daytime nightwear and peel on her new, night-time pyjamas. Soon, she will be ready to be hooked up. To be fed down her swan-like throat via her button-nose into her wizened, concave belly.

Sunday, 8th September 2013.

Helen Anderson posted:
Home! (For now, at least...) Tired but keen for some normality before chemo starts again on Wed (comment applies to me and Georgina!)

Wednesday, 11th September 2013.

Been home. Back again. Been put in the shared bed bay again, rather than in an individual side room. Unsurprisingly, Georgina is upset about this, again, particularly as there seem to be rooms available. We are told that it is about bed management. I make a note to speak to Patient Liaison.

We pull the curtains round the bed, but this doesn't make it private. Fabric curtains cannot block out the muttered discussions, the clicking instruments, and the snap of rubber gloves. The bedpans awaiting disposal in the shared bathroom give clues – way too much information - to all about the state of her insides, when she is so sensitive to the scrutiny she is under from the outside. We are aware of being on display, in the midst of this, the worst of all our times. Georgina refuses to take off her wig, even though she is sweating.

I, too, am upset again. I try to hold it in. This 'bay' is a ward. A ward in a hospital. There is no pretence of a 'hotel-style' stay. Among the boil-washed mint blankets and the wipe-down lockers, there is no pretence of any business other than the poisoning we are all here for. Some patients prefer an old-style environment, we are told.

At home, the wig had its first wash. I held the nylon mesh under the gushing showerhead. I rubbed it gently, like a hairdressing apprentice giving a complimentary scalp massage. I resisted the urge to ask the wig if I could get it a coffee or magazines. I didn't enquire where it was going on its holidays this year.

I blobbed a circle of extra-nourishing-protective-glossing detergent onto the roots punched into its crown. I took care not to get my fingers tangled in the strands. This is a bespoke wig, made of real human hair and styled especially to mimic my daughters long-lost own style. Pat. Be gentle. Soft. Too soft. Ineffective. I rinsed away the half-hearted lather and the wig floated in the bath like a stranded jellyfish.

I wanted to poke it with a stick. I needed tongs like the ones washerwomen used to plunge into wells of steaming carbolic. It wriggled in my hand like the guinea pig I used to have, which sadly got the mange. I smoothed the brittle strands with conditioner which smelled and felt like lemon syllabub. Too impatient to wait the full ten minutes for its magic, I guessed at about eight and it definitely looked better. I rinsed the floppy waves and lifted the hair at the roots to ensure even distribution. The mesh scalp was peachy and translucent. I struggle to keep a grip.

I placed the wet wig on the white polystyrene head I'd ordered off the internet and I brushed through the lengths. The end came off one of the bristles, and I almost took out an eye, scratching the head's scaly skin so that it is scarred like a cartoon pirate's. I switched on the heat. Start gently. Try medium. High. Smoke? I let it dry naturally among the cityscape canvases and the incongruous, retained teddies and the numerous remote controls and the mascara-splashed cream carpet of my daughter's newly decorated, 'grown-up' bedroom, across the landing from her brother's and from ours. I let it dry naturally next to the pile of beanies and bandanas, and the old-lady nylon turban that I ordered off the internet in error because the fabric description was inaccurate.

The lack of privacy goes from bad to worse. We are assigned the 'jolly' nurse, who irritates the life out of Georgina, her dad and me. She is known as the life and soul of the ward and the whole show is all about her - dead and soulless – whenever she is on shift. Anxiety may be making me mean, but it seems to me that when she smiles, it is more like she is baring her teeth in a challenge.

I try not to spread my negativity about her to my daughter, but she looks deflated – completely independently - when the nurse rolls in to announce how lucky we are to have her today. The jolly nurse's unconstrained door slamming reveals her true level of regard for her patient's welfare. Her shoes clack, unconstrained, and her thighs make a noise like fingernails on a blackboard as they rub together in her polyester slacks. The last part, she can't help. I told you anxiety is making me mean. But does every laugh have to be a hoot?

It's hard not to compare your case to the one of the family opposite. You can piece together the 'snatches' through the curtains, even if you don't have a brain for jigsaws. They spell it out and you just hear it, without listening. The girl in the other bed's case isn't as serious as Georgina's, though I know that her mum is beside herself, too. They give us the full lowdown: her outlook is better. She says needles knock her sick. When Georgina's chemo starts again, she will see and hear sick. Maybe she will catch it. They underestimate how contagious nausea is.

There is that awful moment when you realise that you are the family that everyone's glad they're not – that, even by cancer ward standards, you're an object of pity.

Friday, 13th September 2013.

Helen Anderson posted:
Waiting for Georgina to go down to theatre to get her infected Hickman line replaced. We are told it'll be a quick job. Bless her xxxx

Saturday, 14th September 2013.

In trouble again. I went to meet two of Georgina's friends from the station and brought them to the 'quiet room' on the ward, to visit her. We went in without knocking, and she was bald.

She was particularly cross that her male friend had seen her bald. I am the worst mother ever. Her father, who directed me to the room without warning me that she'd taken off her wig to cool off, is still the best daddy ever. She was running late, getting ready, and he didn't want to chivvy her along. He likes to be the good cop. I am banished to the fold-up bed in the shared bay, out of her sight, while she composes herself.

Dear   Diary/Notebook/Journal/Whatever, you are my only friend in this place. Nobody cares if I am despondent, dejected, despairing or depressed. I know it's not about me, but I am so alone. In the midst of this crisis, my husband's love for me has gone out of the (sealed) window, as if he can't care about two people at once. He pops in to tell me that I am disgusting. Yet another 'd' word. It feels like there is not enough love to go round. It is bad enough, thinking about losing her, without him cutting me off, overnight. Add 'desperate' to the list.

At times like this, you find out who your friends are. Mine are far, far away – beyond reach. I think of the sleeping pills in my washbag and of the feel of the soft white powder circles dissolving on my tongue. Not an option. I reach for this white page, instead.

<u>Monday, 16th September 2013.</u>

She is moved to an individual side room and we can enjoy a cuddle in her bed. I try not to let my love handles spill out. I have to pull up the side bars, to contain my out-of-control flesh. My daughter's clammy, fat-stripped limbs rest

26

against my padded body. I am glad that in this way, at least, I am soft. I am a comfort. A mother.

I tuck my chin down, to kiss the top of her head. Jagged new growth pricks my over-chewed bottom lip. I kiss her for longer than either of us would normally prefer, making sure that each prickle is imprinted on me. I sneak a sniff behind her ears. I don't really sneak, because she lets me. She smells of belonging to me. My young. I try to push away the image of a baby bird lying featherless on the pavement.

Georgina says she is too warm. I peel myself off her like a strip of wax. The gap which I leave makes her shiver. A former patient's mum has crafted and donated an amazing pink patchwork quilt for her, and I pull it around her bony, punctured clavicles. Does "a former patient" mean that the child is out of treatment or that he/she no longer exists? This quilt brings great comfort. Like an organ donor, we can't know too much about this woman who has pieced together scraps of the colours of Georgina's life and stitched them to make such a beautiful whole. She has overstitched a floral design: this child, too, is so loved.

I imagine this other mum, crouched over a polished dining table, pulling the squares into the path of the needle. Not daring to stop. Always knowing that there are more of us out there, trying to snuff out icy gaps around our child.

Tuesday, 17th September 2013.

Helen Anderson posted:
Hope Georgina gets her new line put in tomorrow so she can re-start her chemo. She was bumped off the emergency list today but she is being prepped for surgery in the morning.

Wednesday, 18th September 2013.

Helen Anderson posted:
She is back from theatre and sore-but-ok xx

Thursday, 19th September 2013.

Helen Anderson posted:
Georgina's chemo is up and running. Relieved to get on with it.

Friday, 20th September 2013.

Georgina doesn't want me looking at her. "Staring", she calls it. "Gawping".

She wakes up to find me at her bedside, not wanting her to feel alone. I was drinking in her features as she slept. Cataloguing her moist brow; her waxy eyelids; her long lashes – sparse, now. Her pupils are angry as they appear, adjusting to the half-light from the window to the atrium. We don't have an outside view.

I note the snub nose, which is flaking slightly; the well-defined channels from her tiny nostrils to the bow of her top lip; the blue-white, shrivelled bottom lip. She has her dad's chin - she calls it her "bum chin" - with a determined full stop of a dimple. I glance at her smooth, steri-stripped throat.

"What are you staring at?" She is irritated.

"I don't know." There are a thousand replies I should have made, instead. I wonder what she sees, when she looks back at me. I try to hide, but she can see.

Saturday, 21st September 2013.

Sunlight forces its way through the smoked glass roof of the hospital canteen. It's not exactly smoked, in that it's not grey or opaque, but it makes the rays less fierce. Diffuses, them, maybe. There's probably a term for it. On the telly in the ward kitchen, they said we're heading for an autumn heatwave. An Indian summer. Sipping my coffee, I'm sitting in the cloisters of a monastery converted into a hotel. I'm on a cruise ship. In a vast mall. I'm in a bubble. The sun has lost its heat by the time it makes it down to me here.

I hear the people talking about the weather outside. I can't tell, looking up at the glazed, distant heavens. We don't have weather in this place. Just Acts of God.

Tuesday, 24th September 2013.

Helen Anderson shared Paul Anderson's post:

This round of chemo has been pretty awful for Georgina. She didn't even have the strength to watch TV or go on her phone!! Unbelievable, for any teenager, I know!! lol.

She's not been able to eat or drink for quite a few days which doesn't help. We're not sure of the exact plan, as it will depend on an MRI scan organised for Thursday. Surgery will follow at some point, on the main tumour, on the liver, plus more chemo and then possibly radiotherapy.

As usual, she's been very determined, battling through it all. She showed some signs of hopefully picking up last night and managed a bit of a laugh with the nurses.

Thursday, 26th September 2013.

I know that I need to write. I need to empty the silt from my head and purge this anxiety. But what to write? I think about new characters – all the new people I have met recently. Professionals. Parents. Teenagers. Baldy children. All the baldy little babies who haven't yet had chance to sprout hair to lose.

I think about the ferocity of the mothers of the patients. Women who wouldn't normally say 'boo' to a goose stand on guard, checking and double-checking the medication which is offered to their young. They question the consultants with printouts from the internet or articles ripped from the Daily Mail by their mother-in-law. They demand answers, where there are none.

We flap like female blackbirds distracting a fat, black cat from the tender morsels of chick in the nest. We squawk "Take me, instead" but the menacing shadow looms larger, as we anticipate the direction in which it will pounce, next. Cats strike when you least expect it, pinning their claws into you and rubbing their scent on you.

Leaving you smelling like a crazy cat lady, no matter how many times you wash yourself and your clothes. As if my black dog isn't bad enough.

How do you work on a children's oncology ward and keep cheerful? Do the nurses lock themselves in the linen cupboard and cry into the rubberised pillows? Does the sadness rub against you until a callous forms? I think about the nurses' jokes and penchant for pranks: how do they judge when it's just really not a laughing matter? Are any subjects off limits? Sister has a policy on everything. What is Sister's policy on black humour?

I need to go home for a bit. I have a son, too, and he won't be there forever. London is calling him back. I need to change my clothes - to find a new selection of tops-and-jeans combos, to rotate for as long as it takes. I used to like this blouse I am wearing. I liked its violet on aqua on cobalt. Its middling weight. The geometric pattern. Black, grey, white. I hadn't considered all its colours, until now. I have stared at it so long that it's giving off an aura. There is a ghost-print of jagged green zigzags, when I finally rest my eyes on the bare white wall.

Tuesday, 1st October 2013.

I did not go home. She was not well enough to leave.

It is October already. It was only just September when I packed for this hospital stay and I haven't brought a coat. When I packed for this trip, I'd only just swapped my sandals for ballerina pumps. Now, in the parents'

31

accommodation over the road from A & E, they've got the heating on full blast. I can't turn it off, because it's centrally controlled, so I open the top window. I am scared that a bogeyman will climb in during the night and get me. I wear pyjamas in case there's a fire and I sweat buckets, with the duvet covering one side of my body.

This room is sponsored by a charity called Jodie's Journey. It's kind of them to put a roof over my head, but I'm not sure whether I want to travel with Jodie. I'm not sure which way she went and I daren't ask. Why couldn't I have been allocated the one sponsored by the Freemasons? You know where you are with their secret handshakes.

Today, I let the students in the dental hospital next door practise pulling out teeth. I thanked them for the hole where the pain and the puffiness have been and I meant it. I am glad to be rid of the root which has been doggedly rotting while I couldn't get away to see my own dentist. I hope the feeling never returns to my cheek.

I think of my daughter's adult-sized school shoes, worn for two days. It's not the money that I mind. We have not had good news, today, from Georgina's consultant. I know each vein and freckle on the forearms which protrude from his rolled-up sleeves. He still has a watch strap mark, left over from his summer holidays in America with his wife and girls. I kept my eyes fixed on it while he spoke. Once, I dared let my attention wander to his face, but I did not like the words that I saw coming out of his mouth. I quickly switched back to that blank, cream stripe with a single golden mole where time should be ticking.

Wednesday, 2nd October 2013.

Helen Anderson posted:
Second visit to dental hospital for me this week. Trying to be a brave soldier, given what Gg has been putting up with recently!

Thursday, 3rd October 2013.

The pain is creeping back into the ragged tooth socket that the students so meticulously irrigated and packed. Every night when I settle down to try to sleep; I think that it will all have sorted itself out by morning. That the swelling will have disappeared. Every day, the swelling is more and more obvious, from the outside. I can see my own nose, distorted. My cheek has puffed up into my line of vision. Each pulse brings more pain. I pop pills – full of promises – but they kill nothing. They are full of shit. This situation is making me mean.

I would put on a brave face, only I can't find it. Maybe the bogeyman did creep in through the top window during the night. Maybe the bogeyman has nabbed my brave face, although it's strange that he left my iPhone behind and all the jewellery on the sink. What a stupid place to leave my jewellery. Things can so easily go straight down the plughole. In a flash. Without any warning whatsoever – never mind a three minute one. Three minutes isn't very long, except when you're in agony. It's not even time enough to write your bucket list. It's not even time to formulate the thought that you should write one.

Wednesday, 6th October 2013.

Helen Anderson shared Paul Anderson's post:
The MRI showed the chemo wasn't working and as the cancer is very rare, there isn't a standard alternative chemo.
Georgina is willing to try anything to fight this, so today she has started on a new chemo that is used for similar cancers.
She is still in good spirits and has been incredible. Despite a bit of pain recently, Georgina has had a few nice days, seeing friends and even teachers!!

Wednesday, 6th October 2013.

Helen Anderson posted:
Some lovely huggles with my funny, brave girl this weekend. Also nice to see some of her friends and have a laugh with Sarah Henderson xxxx

Monday, 7th October 2013.

In the coffee bar, next to Patient Liaison. I am eating a large hunk of blueberry and vanilla cake. It's sweet. Moist. It sticks to the ridges of my palate and my gaping gum wound. It's not quite as nice as it looks.

I think of Georgina's consultant, shuffling around her bed. Not quite in charge. I think about his valiant efforts to take an interest in her nail-art, and the way that her Beyoncé paper dress-up doll seemed to flummox him. It seems as if he's not quite sure what tone to take: how to strike a fun-but-the-right-side-of-appropriate tone. I imagine him with his daughters, at home. I wonder if he looks at Georgina and sees their faces. I wonder if he looks at his daughter and thinks about Georgina, and all the other girls before her.

The cake is gone. I must be the one who ate it. The coffee is brown, like oxtail soup. Substantial. It tastes better than it looks. I read about Jodie, of Jodie's Journey, on Facebook. She's up for an award for her courage. I digest her details. Eighteen. Incurable. Life-limiting. This doesn't seem such a bad destination. Crazy, but it's all relative. But she can never eat again – she has to have the nutrients pumped straight into her heart. That'll be via a Hickman line. I know these words. She blogs and she has a website and she raises money to help others. I click 'Like' and 'Follow'.

Sunday, 13th October 2013.

Serious meeting with the consultant who is in charge over the weekend. She confirms that I am not imagining it all. That the worries that I've been whispering to my husband as we take over each other's watch aren't merely pessimistic catastrophising. Paul looks desperate, as if he's being told bad news for the first time. We cling on to hope.

This doctor says we need to be thinking ahead, even if we are keeping on hoping. She has a pretty name for a person doling out such ghastly advice. I fix on a grey hair poking out from the front of her parting. It is growing in exactly the same place as my own wiriest, whitest hair. Tomorrow, if we get home, I will attempt to cover mine, one last time, with semi-permanent berry red. If it fails to take, I may have to give up and let the salt and pepper turn saltier. Who am I kidding, anyway? Everybody knows nobody has hair so unfeasibly bright – not all of the time.

This doctor's voice sinks lower than low. She has kind, brown, unswerving eyes. She won't let my husband wriggle back into his world of wishing it all away. It is Sunday afternoon, and she is wearing casual, stone-washed red slacks. Her necklace consists of green discs – perhaps shells, perhaps seed pods – threaded onto black cord. It is no-nonsense and un-glitzy as it distracts the children and the babies from her prodding and poking and pronouncing upon. It is something for me to pin my panic to. In spite of myself, I like this doctor. In spite of what she says to us.

Georgina is turning yellow. Simpson-yellow. Custard. She has sallow cheeks and eyeballs. I wish that I could wheel my daughter into the sun. I wish I could stick her under UV lights, like when she was jaundiced as a baby. I wish that I could just slide her into an incubator, naked, and shield her eyes while the rays heal her. All I can do is reach under her covers to offer my hand for my daughter to hold, just as I pushed my finger through the incubator porthole for my newborn to grasp. In those days, I knew how to pacify her. Those were early days. Shiny. New.

Monday, 14th October 2013.

Helen Anderson posted:
My one-sided hamster-face thing is back.
Been back to the dental hospital for much prodding
and photographing and puzzling. More antibiotics?
Ta v much

Tuesday, 15th October 2013.

Helen Anderson posted:
Trying to remember all the things I'm meant
to pick up on my flying visit home, but it seems
that my brain has turned to marmalade (shredded,
if you're interested) can't remember where things
are kept: it has been 5 weeks since I was here.

Monday, 18th October 2013.

Helen Anderson posted:
Nice day yesterday with visits from
Georgina's friends (courtesy of teachers acting
industrially) and a trip with G to see 'We're the
Millers' courtesy of Medicinema.

Saturday, 19th October 2013.

Shopping for Georgina's 15th birthday. I
want to buy all of the contents of Fenwick. I could
buy her all of Fenwick and John Lewis and it still
wouldn't be enough. There is no compensation
huge enough for this cancer.

I sit by her bedside, listening to her
breathing. It is slow. Later, the nurse tells us that
it had been eleven resps per minute. That is not

enough - that much I know. My daughter mumbles in her sleep. She makes kitten-cries. I want to wake her – to shake her out of her bad dreams. Yet I don't want to wake her to this reality which is even worse.

My head feels like it's underwater. I listen, hard, but my own heartbeat fills my ears. It is fast. My knees feel like I've just swum the length of Windermere, like Georgina's challenge-loving science teacher, Miss Bell. But they forgot to send a boat to accompany me, and I've never been out of the baby pool before. These are different waters. Icy. Bottomless. Vicious. Shifting currents pull me back where I started, no matter which strokes I use. I haven't been taught past front crawl. I can't see underwater. I can't even open my eyes, so I don't know how I know that I can't see.

Georgina lets me sniff behind her ears, when I kiss her goodnight. I try not to, because she doesn't like it. She knows I want to.

"You're allowed to sniff."

I breathe in. Cinnamon. Spice. Salt. Hot in my nostrils. I hold her there, humid. I don't want to exhale. It takes me four attempts to leave the ward tonight. I almost turn round again, but a doctor is holding the door open. He looks so young, dressed in his blue-shirt-cream-chinos doctor's outfit.

I forgot to dye my hair, when I popped home. I didn't forget, really. I hadn't the heart. I'm showing my age. Like rings on a tree, you can work it out by the colours of my roots. From above, my scalp has a pink halo and a grey inner circle. There is a strip of defenceless, melanin-free white, at the core. My scalp burns easily, but I won't be seeing the sun again for a while.

Words are not coming to me so easily. Or rather, they come to mind but lodge firmly in my carpal tunnel. They stay wedged, refusing to transmit to the plastic shell of my propelling pencil. I have bought a multi-pack from a supermarket. A well-known brand-name, nonetheless.

Today, Georgina wanted me to promise not to kill myself, if she dies.

"I'm not planning to. I'm planning to be strong for your dad and your brother." I mean all of this, though I won't make false, absolute promises.

Now, I need to make sure that my plan comes together.

Sunday, 20th October 2013.

Helen Anderson posted:
Quick update on G xxx
Helen Anderson shared Paul Anderson's post:
It's Georgina's 15th birthday on Tuesday!! She's had a lot of friends to visit recently, which is much appreciated.

Family are coming today and then on Tuesday she is going to see Arctic Monkeys at Newcastle Arena. Next scan is Friday afternoon. She's in a lot of discomfort, but the morphine controls it. She remains in good spirits and is a very brave young lady.

Monday, 21st October 2013.

The eve of my daughter's fifteenth birthday. I have held myself together, to buy the cake. The wrapping paper. The banners. I wrestle with a funny mix of sadness and happiness as I wash and scrunch-dry Georgina's wig, ready for her birthday outing. I hold it together some more. A bit longer.

A lady comes to the ward to offer massages to parents and patients. She tells me that I have a very special young lady. Georgina is so grown-up, discussing meridian lines and complementary therapies with great authority. She is a vision in the pink print pyjamas and pink fluffy slippers her friends, Lauren and Mia, brought at the weekend as an early birthday present. She is a daughter to be proud of. My daughter.

She has touched lives. I want to avoid such clichés but they're repeated with good reason. I don't want to use the past tense, to talk about my daughter. Not now. Not ever. I stretch out the tiny scrap of future left in my hands. I gauge its tensile strength. I feel it give.

Tuesday, 22nd October 2013.

Helen Anderson posted:
Happy 15th birthday to my wonderful daughter, who is currently snoozing in preparation for tonight's gig. Xxxxxxxxxxxxxxxx

Helen Anderson posted:
Well, Georgina and her friends and Paul made it to the Arena. She looked gorgeous but

didn't want photos taken. Paul is under instructions to blend into the background. Strictly no dad-dancing!

Wednesday, 23rd October 2013.

Helen Anderson posted:
A day of rest after yesterday's excitement. Thanks to everyone who made G's birthday extra-special (including the doctor who stayed back 2 hours after her shift ended, to check G was ok) xxx

Wednesday, 23rd October 2013.

Georgina is fifteen years and one day old. I scribble down everything that I can remember about her birthday.

I woke up alone in the parents' accommodation. I got dressed as quickly as I could, but by the time I got to the ward, her teacher had already had the whole school on speakerphone in assembly, singing Happy Birthday to Georgina. Ed Sheeran – along with thousands of others - had listened to Georgina's beautiful cover of 'I Can't Make You Love Me' on YouTube.

She had had a tiring night, watched over by her dad. I sat in her hospital room, as they both slept through the morning. My daughter awoke and opened some presents. There was more sleeping, then piles of post. My daughter is a polite girl, reading the cards first. We had put up Birthday Girl banners and pink balloons. I pinned a fuchsia bow on her pillow. All her presents were double-wrapped in sparkle.

41

She asked us to display the presents on our fold-down bed. She seemed delighted with the DKNY bag and the Benefit brow pencil and the Urban Decay eyeshadow. She is a designer junkie, my designer baby. She asked us to take photos of the presents, but she wouldn't let us get her in the picture.

Georgina's phone bleeped and vibrated on the table next to the bed. She 'blocked' her Facebook wall, so that she wouldn't be overwhelmed with posts, but some circumvented this by 'tagging' her. All that love: she could feel it buzzing, even if she couldn't face another message about keeping on fighting. Sometimes, having the crowd cheering you on gives you strength, but sometimes the support brings panic-inducing pressure.

In the afternoon, the staff gathered at the foot of her bed. From Georgina's consultant, through to the domestics, they sang "Happy Birthday, Georgina" together. The ward staff gave my daughter a Jack Wills bag and a Jack Wills bracelet. More logos. The joy of logos.

There was a cake with candles in the shapes of a 'one' and a 'five'. We couldn't light them because of the smoke alarms but I could almost see them glow. Then, we lay together in that hospital bed – my daughter and I – cuddling. I twitched to sleep and nearly fell out. I lay there, registering her breath and memorising the pattern of the golden down on her head.

When it was time for her to get ready for the Arctic Monkeys gig, she forced her swollen feet into the black leather boots which used to fit. There was relief that her new silver vest top draped over her bump. Bump. Hump. Tumour. The designer eyeshadow was applied according to instructions given in an internet tutorial. My husband was tasked with applying glue to false eyelashes. We were all learning, all the time. It was decided that the tousled wig looked like a caveman's, so I set about straightening and sleeking.

Georgina's friends, Beth and Callum, had tickets, too, and they came to meet her at the hospital. They got lost in the old wing. Time was ticking, so the registrar raced along the passageways in her high heels, to track them down. She saved the day. We wheeled Georgina to the main entrance. The cold air hit her - the first time in six weeks that she had left the building. The cheerful Geordie taxi-driver zoomed her up the ramp into the adapted taxi and strapped her in. She looked afraid of being out of control. Maybe that's me, projecting. She and her friends smiled and waved as they eased out of the hospital gates and hit the Geordie traffic.

I sat in the ward kitchen with the other mothers. I listened to their tales about their children's cancers. I couldn't find a story less hopeful than ours. I didn't say a thing, and then worried about what the other mothers would think of me. I can't believe I was still bothered about what people might think. I phoned my mum. I shifted Georgina's presents off the fold-up bed and lay still, under Georgina's bright pink, birthday-present, fleece throw.

The registrar stuck her head around the door, to see if I'd heard from them. This doctor had stayed back two hours after the end of her official shift, to make sure Georgina could get her medication as soon as she came back. I checked my texts again. Okay. Everybody okay. When Georgina returned, she was too tired to step out of her wheelchair. We peeled off the lashes and left the rest of her make-up on. So shoot us. We wiggled off those boots and lifted her into bed. Lorazepam was administered. Heat packs were applied. It was worth it. She did it. We did it.

Saturday, 26th October 2013.

Helen Anderson posted:
Sorry to deliver this news on Facebook but it is the most efficient way of contacting all the people who have been asking about Georgina. Yesterday's scan showed that her cancer has spread and can't be treated. So the focus will be on getting her pain-free and at home. Georgina wants to stay strong and happy and hopes we can all support her in this xxxxx

Sunday, 27th October 2013.

Helen Anderson posted:
Please share this link to Georgina's YouTube video and don't forget to view it on YouTube, too. We are trying to get G as many views as possible!! Thank you x

Helen Anderson posted:
Thanks to everyone viewing Georgina's cover of Bonnie Raitt's 'I Can't Make You Love Me' on YouTube. Your support means a lot (sounding like an X Factor person now - time for bed!!!) x

Thursday, 31st October 2013.

Helen Anderson posted:
Coming home soon x

Paul Anderson posted:
Georgina had an interesting day today. My cousin Peter and his lovely wife Debbie came to visit this morning. Pete's nearly as daft as me so that was fun. Georgina loved seeing them.

Georgina was then interviewed by TFM radio about her YouTube hit and her music. It should be on air tomorrow morning.

This afternoon Georgina received an unexpected signed CD from The Arctic Monkeys! Wow!!

Ed Sheeran is trying to get in touch with her!! Double wow!!!

And we were told we can go home tomorrow!!!! Bit scary after 7 weeks, but looking forward to Georgina being able to see her family and friends.

Friday, 1st November 2013.

Helen Anderson posted:
I think Metro/TFM Radio did a good job for Georgina today. The reporters were lovely and handled the situation sensitively xx proud mum xx

Helen Anderson posted:
Georgina's voice is being heard!! Xx please keep sharing xxx

Helen Anderson posted:

Lovely snuggles with my girl, plus having my boy home — feeling good.

Friday, 1st November 2013.

Focusing on Georgina's music and seeing the number of views on her YouTube video is giving us a positive distraction from Georgina's illness. So many kind messages and people spreading the word. Her dream has always been for the world to hear her sing. But what awful circumstances under which to fulfil that dream.

Saturday, 2nd November 2013.

Helen Anderson posted:
72,854 views, including Gary Numan and John Bishop!

Sunday, 3rd November 2013.

Helen Anderson posted:
Flowers and chocs for Georgina from James Arthur — feeling special.

Friday, 8th November 2013.

Helen Anderson posted:
I agree with Paul Anderson, who just posted:
So much support from so many people. Georgina says she is very happy with the response and when I asked her what she thought of the number of views, she said "very good!" She is content, the world has heard her. Thank you xx

Saturday, 9th November 2013.

Paul Anderson posted:
What a day!!
Georgina was incredibly brave and managed to get to the Boro match as a VIP guest of honour, despite feeling incredibly ill, with discomfort from the cancer. It was a fantastic day! Yvonne Ferguson and Middlesbrough FC ensured we were looked after, with every minute detail being planned out perfectly. Neil Bauser taking time to chat to us was also special.

Jonathan Woodgate escorted Georgina, Helen and me onto the centre circle in Georgina's wheelchair, totally against all rules! A dream come true for ME!! Players waved to her in person, including Kei Kamara and Rhys Williams.

Then to top it all they played Georgina's OWN song, 'Two Thirds of a Piece,' before the match and at half-time. When the crowd applauded in front of us, without knowing Georgina was there, it was a beautiful memory.

We had to leave early (a first for me!) as Georgina was exhausted, but Neil Bauser went out of his way to make sure a DVD of the match found its way to me!

What a fantastic club and they said no publicity please, but stuff that!! Thank you, Boro.

Saturday, 9th November 2013.

Georgina's version of Bonnie Raitt's 'I Can't Make You Love Me' has now had more than 154,000 hits on YouTube - in the space of just two weeks.

Sunday, 10th November 2013.

Helen Anderson posted:
Georgina had a rough night but yet again astounded us all by responding when actress Melanie Hill called in to wish her well and give her Waterloo Road goodies, including a signed script, school tie and a 'Head Girl' badge!! What a lovely lady Melanie is - really easy to talk to. And how fab my girl is (sorry for repeating myself a lot in this way, lately. Bear with me!!) xx Watching G sleep now xx

Monday, 11th November 2013.

Paul Anderson uploaded a new video from 11 November 2013 to his Timeline:
Wow Olly Murs! Thank you! Georgina

Thursday, 14th November 2013.

Helen Anderson posted:
Thank you for all the good wishes and love being sent to us. Georgina died peacefully in the early hours of this morning, cuddled by her mum and holding her dad's hand. Her body had just got too weary, even though she was such a determined young lady. Paul and I are so proud of our brave daughter. We are finding strength in the support being shown to us and trying to follow her example in staying strong for one another, as she expressly said that she didn't want those she was leaving behind to be sad. Although we are devastated by her loss, we are happy that she has touched so many lives and will live on in the

thoughts and memories of her friends, family and the whole community xxxxx

Friday, 15th November 2013.

Andy Passant, of the Evening Gazette, wrote:

Georgina Anderson: Crowd gathers in Marske for poignant tribute to 'the brightest star in the sky'.

Hundreds of people braved the winter chill on the seafront at Marske to remember popular schoolgirl Georgina Anderson.

Friends of Georgina Anderson met on the Coast Road in Marske to release lanterns and balloons in her memory.

Hundreds turned out for a poignant tribute to "the brightest star in the sky".

A massive crowd gathered in Marske last night to remember 15-year-old Georgina Anderson.

Lanterns were lit and released into the sky in memory of the gifted singer whose music and brave battle against cancer touched many hearts. Many hundreds of people braved the winter chill on the seafront at Marske to remember the popular schoolgirl.

Those who knew and loved Georgina were united in grief with others who had never met her but wanted to pay their respects.

Despite the windy conditions, people persevered and cheered as lanterns were lit and floated away into the night sky, with Georgina's music being played from cars providing a fitting backdrop. Fighting back tears, one of her friends,

13-year-old Georgia Dixon, said: "She is the brightest star in the sky."

Georgia added: "It is absolutely amazing how many people have turned up. She is going to be looking down on us all thinking we have done her proud."

Nicole Hill, who joined the throng last night, said she was Georgina's PE teacher at Bydales. She said: "All Georgina wanted was people to be happy, smiling and celebrate her life. She was just a warm-hearted, fantastic young lady. She was well-liked by everybody, pupils, staff." One woman said she didn't know Georgina but had heard her music.

She said: "It is just so sad that she hasn't been able to fulfil that talent but I am glad that people have got the chance to hear her music. I think it has just touched everybody."

Phillip Boseley, from Boosbeck, who was there with his family, said: "We had seen it on Facebook and we had listened to her music on YouTube. We just wanted to pay our respects. I can't believe she was at Middlesbrough football match on Saturday and she has gone so quick."

Many tributes were also paid on Facebook and Twitter, including tweets from fellow Teesside music talents James Arthur and Abi Alton. On Facebook, people spoke of Georgina as "an inspiration" who had brought happiness to the world through her music and who was now "singing in heaven with the angels".

One described her as "a brave beautiful young girl with an amazing voice" while another said: "You'll be forever in the sunset and sunrise over the sea views from Marske."

People also gathered at the Infinity Bridge in Stockton, where lanterns were also released in her memory.

Monday, 18th November 2013.

Published in the Evening Gazette:
Obituary
ANDERSON Georgina Louise
Peacefully at home in the arms of her mum and dad on November 14, Georgina aged 15 years of Marske. Precious daughter of Helen and Paul, loved sister of Joe, adored grand-daughter of Keith and the late Betty, and of Margaret and the late Colin. Also a treasured niece and cousin.

Funeral service to take place on Friday, November 22 at 2p.m. in St. Mark's Church, Marske prior to private committal service. Family and friends please meet at church, and at Georgina's request wear something pink. Family flowers only, donations in lieu to the Teenage Cancer Trust and Cancer Research U.K.

Monday, 18th November 2013.

Laura Love, of the Evening Gazette, wrote:
Georgina Anderson passed away peacefully in her parents' arms just hours after hearing the news that one of her own songs was to be released as a single

The heartbroken family of Georgina Anderson today paid tribute to their "beautiful girl, inside and out".

Georgina passed away peacefully in her parents' arms last Thursday - just four months after being diagnosed with an extremely rare and aggressive form of cancer "Everybody I have spoken to have all said they have no words but there isn't anything that anyone can say," said her dad Paul.

"The love and warmth we are receiving is fantastic but obviously it is still very hard when you are grieving for your 15-year-old daughter."

Georgina from Marske was diagnosed with stage four liver cancer, which had spread to her lungs in July. The Year 10 Bydales School pupil underwent chemotherapy but last month doctors at Newcastle's Royal Victoria Infirmary said that there were no other treatment options available.

A talented musician, Georgina, daughter of Paul and Helen, 45, had a lifelong dream of having her music heard across the globe.

And before she passed away, she was able to see her version of Bonnie Raitt's I Can't Make You Love Me go viral on YouTube.

One of her self-penned songs, Two Thirds of a Piece, was also released the day before she died.

Yesterday, it entered the UK singles chart at number 63.

"Georgina knew that the single was going to be released," said Paul, 46. "She was very pleased and excited about it but by that stage she was very, very ill."

Georgina died just hours after hearing the news. "She died at home in our arms peacefully," said Paul.

"The last three weeks of her life were exciting for her," he added. "She was in a lot of pain but

never moaned once. She got some enjoyment out of a very difficult situation."

On Saturday, November 9, Georgina, her parents, brother Joe, 20, and two of her friends travelled to Middlesbrough's Riverside Stadium to hear Two Thirds of a Piece played out twice to the crowd.

"She was desperate to go to the Middlesbrough match and she had a wonderful day," said Paul. "It was unbelievable - those are the words she used. She was sat in the executive box looking out on the big crowd listening to her music blasting out. She said 'this is unbelievable'. It was beautiful. But it is hard to comprehend how on Saturday she was here and heard her single aired in public for the first time and then on Thursday she passed away."

Paul said Georgina was also "thrilled to bits" to speak to James Arthur, as well as getting video messages from the cast of Waterloo Road, Olly Murs and Ed Sheeran.

Celebrities such as Simon Cowell have also been tweeting on her behalf, and James Arthur dedicated his Children in Need performance to her.

"The celebrity endorsements were just the icing on the cake," said Paul "All she wanted was for her music to be heard and for some good to come out of it." Paul and his family now want to "thank everyone for their overwhelming support".

"The local community and the whole of Teesside have come together to support us," he said.

Hundreds of people gathered in Marske last Thursday to light lanterns in Georgina's memory.

"We couldn't face going to the lantern release but we watched it from a distance and it was heart-warming," said Paul. "Georgina would have been looking down with a smile on her face. She would have also been having a bit of a laugh seeing everyone trying to light the lanterns."

"For everybody, it puts life into perspective. It makes people realise what life should be about and that is what Georgina would have wanted. She was a beautiful girl inside and out. She was a very kind girl, very compassionate, and very forthright in her views. We were very proud of her for that."

He added: "We just want her message to reach far and wide and if some good can come out of it then that would be great."

Two Thirds of a Piece is available on iTunes and on Google Play. The proceeds will be shared between the Teenage Cancer Trust and Cancer Research.

The Sick Children's Trust, Clic Sargent and Macmillan were also causes close to Georgina's heart and funds will hopefully be raised for those charities in the future.

Georgina's funeral will take place on Friday at St Mark's Church in Marske.

<u>Monday, 18th November 2013.</u>

Helen Anderson posted:
I think Georgina would have been pleased to be next to Taylor Swift in the Official UK Charts xxxx

Wednesday, 20th November 2013.

Helen Anderson posted:
Been going through photos of Georgina: don't
know whether to laugh or cry, so I should probably
go to bed!

Thursday, 21st November 2013.

The day before Georgina's funeral. Just
when you think that you've covered all angles,
more questions pop up. More questions about the
detail of the arrangements. More questions with
no answers.

I have been comfort-eating the chocolates
that came with Georgina's flowers from James
Arthur. We visit the hotel where we will hold the
wake. I have to decide whether pink organza bows
on the dining chairs are OTT. I am telling myself
that it doesn't matter, but this is the party which
will replace Georgina's sixteenth and eighteenth
birthdays and the wedding that will never be. I
need to get this funeral and wake right. It's the
least that I can do when I couldn't find a doctor to
save her.

We create a slideshow for them to screen in
the corner of the function room. We deliberate
over the timing of the interval between each snap
in the slideshow of her life. The slides are fading
in and out too abruptly, teasing your memory
then disappearing. I wish that my daughter's life
could be put on a constant loop.

It is tea-time and it is dark. Fairy lights twist
along the beams of the hotel conservatory roof,
welcome twinkles against mourning. I am glad

when the owner suggests candles. They have thought about Georgina's spirit, although it can't be captured in a table setting. Attention to all these details doesn't make things right, but I feel confident that I'm not making things more wrong. Can you have 'more wrong'? 'Wronger'? I feel that we will be in safe hands, here. We might be able to keep Georgina close to us for a little while longer.

Today is my niece's twelfth birthday. She has come north, for her cousin's funeral. She looks sheepish to be celebrating. To have lived another year. I ask her about her birthday-treat visit to the Harry Potter Studios. She tells me, and cuddles in. Her corkscrew blonde curls are so different from Georgina's straight brown hair. Her head is so different from my daughter's prickly dome, with its undisguised fault lines where the plates in her skull had somehow shifted and failed to knit back together. I hold my niece gently, as I used to hold my daughter. Trying not to squash her tumour, which strained through her bruised skin, clashing against my middle-age spread. I chance a subtle sniff. My niece does not have the precise odour of one of my young. But she is warm. She is alive.

Yesterday, as Paul and I drove back from viewing our daughter's body in the Chapel of Rest, platinum streaked through a pewter sky. The shafts of sunlight raining down on us were so like a Children's Bible illustration that I almost expected to see God peeping out, complete with piercing eyes and a snow-white beard. We have a few questions for God. He was afraid to show his face, perhaps. But that November sky spoke to us. Hope spoke. I hope that there are good reasons for all this, which have yet to be revealed. If I believed in signs, I would believe in those sunbeams. We almost missed the turn-off, because we were so struck by them. We almost ended up in a ditch.

<u>Monday, 25th November 2013.</u>

A quiet day. Empty. My son went back to university in London. My daughter did not come back. I try to remember how I used to fill my time, before, when I had it. I have too much time to spare. I am going spare. I used to feel irritated by people who found time to crush candy or build farms on their mobile phones. As I play my word game on the tiny screen, I look for meaning amongst the jiggling alphabet tiles. I beat my own top score, but victory is hollow. It is all loss.

<u>Thursday, 28th November 2013.</u>

I have the house to myself. How will I behave when nobody's watching? I think that I trust myself: I have this page.

The candles that I lit for my girl are burning down on the hearth. The pillars of wax curl over, threatening to drown the wicks in a clear pool. I wonder whether the china candle-plates are heatproof. You can't take anything for granted. There is danger, everywhere, on top of the danger of emotion.

On the floor next to the fireplace stands a glittery shoebox, filled with cards of sympathy and condolence. Its lid is propped open, like a custom-made coffin. The cardboard, too, will deteriorate like the skin on my daughter's cheek, in time. For now, I still have them – the messages of love. The proof that she made a difference. Past tense. I fret that they may be too close to the flames.

I read through this diary to date, and wish it were more complete. I wonder how it would look, fleshed out. No missing bones. Each and every cell present and correct. But there have been so many days when it would have been dishonest of me to write. It would have been disingenuous to pore over, in real time, the details of that terrible, final scan. The defeat of the journey home in an ambulance. The steel hospital bed in our downstairs extension. The night that the room where I write became the room where she died. Having her body taken out of the house, wrapped in that pink fleece throw, under cover of darkness, so that the children going to school wouldn't bump into the undertakers. The news reaching Twitter even before school opened and before her friends could be told. The best laid plans.... Plans are what we make while life does whatever it likes, just because it can.

This diary, though incomplete, still bears testament to all that.

Sunday, 1st December 2013.

Helen Anderson posted:
So proud that Middlesbrough Football Club played Georgina's song again at half-time today, and touched that they paid tribute to her in the match programme. They really have gone the extra

mile to support us. I am almost becoming a footie/Boro fan!

Monday, 2nd December 2013.

Mondays aren't great. You have the whole week stretching before you. I try reassuring myself that my life has purpose by checking my calendar. There are tenuous, pencilled –in engagements. (I have also written this journal in pencil, to give myself the option of rubbing myself out). Meet for coffee. Hairdressers. Dentist. Meet for lunch. I don't know what I'll have to say to these people, except "I met X for coffee" and "I met Y for lunch".

I need to go and get Georgina's ashes from the funeral parlour. This doesn't make for polite or cheery conversation. I don't want to become a social leper. People only put up with misery for so long. She has been dead for eighteen days. Only eighteen days. I don't want to collect my daughter's ashes, even if they will be in a rose-bedecked, cardboard, pink tube with a sprinkle-top. I cannot bear to say goodbye again. How many more goodbyes will there be? I can see a lifetime of them – of fleeting recognition evaporating into dust and pain.

I put on the news, so that I will have something to talk about.

Tuesday, 3rd December 2013.

Dark evenings. I am clunking from one nanosecond to the next. So much experienced and endured, but so little time on the clock to show for it. I feel as if someone's playing 'hangman' with me – building up the gallows one stick at a time and dangling me from it. Only attaching my limbs so that I can be chopped down.

I keep on lighting candles. There will be soot on the lounge walls, like the brown tobacco stains when we moved in. I remember the fingernail crescents impressed into the polystyrene coving, as if the previous children of the house had been clinging onto the ceiling like mini-Spidermen. I picture the Kylie and Jason stickers cleaving to the skewed wardrobe doors, which might have been 'fitted' once, but which we easily ripped out in our keenness to erase their family's hold on this time-space.

What mark will our family have left on this house? The blinds have been stripped from the windows and our children were never climbers. The flat porch roof is now pitched. We have added a lawn, a block-paved drive, a kitchen-diner and the writing/dying room.

Wednesday, 4th December 2013.

Helen Anderson posted:
Paul and I will not be celebrating Christmas (at least not in the conventional sense) this year. So, instead of sending cards, we will be making a donation to The Sick Children's Trust. We trust that our friends will understand xxx

Monday, 9th December 2013.

I have been sleeping all afternoon, to pass time which stops and starts in apnoeic fits. I desperately need to arrange things for the new year. I remind myself that this loss of will is an annual occurrence – a seasonal ailment - notwithstanding the death of my daughter. This time last year, only the thought of five days in January alone up a cliff with my dog and my internet-less computer and a suitcase full of notebooks got me through the festivities.

There is an unmistakeable ache to this point in the winter. It's like the flu, when you're not yet over the worst. It's like post-viral fatigue in-the-making.

I have argued with Paul because I wanted to walk alone. I wanted to be alone with the dog and the darkness. Paul wanted to come with me, holding my hand around these gridded streets. I don't like touching. He ended up walking the dog alone, when all he wanted was for our hands to hold. Mondays are the worst. Tea-times are the worst, when Georgina should be home from school. It is Monday – almost tea-time. I curl up on the sofa and I wrap a blanket around the hollows which cover my kidneys.

Last winter, up that cliff, alone, I fell. The sickening crack as my over-aged hand-bones shattered. I am an extra-slow knitter, now. My sister tried to teach me the art of crochet, but my injury stopped me maintaining the tension. The cold makes my forefinger ache, like this ache of midwinter. I remember the thrilled terror of shutting that cottage door behind me as the snow fell, too. Of drawing the curtains and eking out the logs, knowing that I was about to be stranded. I remember my husband coming to dig me out. Forging through the blizzard like Captain Scott. The frustration of having to be rescued. The relief at being saved.

The Pain is a sobering souvenir of The Fall. It's hard to describe – it's not a twinge or a throb or a stab. It refuses to be categorised or graded. It comes and goes, constantly. I've had physio: did my exercises religiously, but I think God knows I'm a non-believer. I still haven't got a full range of movement. It may be pessimistic of me, but I don't think I'll ever knit back together, properly. Maybe my sister will crochet for me. It's something else Georgina will never have the chance to master.

Living vicariously through your children is a dangerous strategy to adopt, anyway, given that children are so prone to accidents and cellular mutations. When they stop breathing, your tissues necrotise, too. When they donate their corneas, you lose sight. When they go up in flames and are stuffed, as ashes, into a tube ready to be scattered, so are you. Just waiting for a blustery sunrise to carry you away. When they leave you, one way or another, you will have left yourself. You'll be caught between your non-self and their departing body, trying to steer clear of the brightness at the end of the black, sucking void.

As Georgina lay dying, we told her that she could go. As her breathing slowed and I squished next to her and her dad held her hand, I suggested that she take a yellow cab to Times

Square. To head for the Broadway lights and to cast her eyes upwards, among the soaring towers. To float away over the Manhattan skyline, like I'd promised her we would for her eighteenth birthday celebrations. I told my daughter that she should go on ahead without us. That we'd be fine. We'd be strong. I made terrible, impossible promises. My daughter got her birthday wish, three years early. We had to let her come of age, too soon. We had to give her to the city of her dreams.

Tuesday, 10th December 2013.

People ask how I'm doing and I talk about myself, using stock phrases. I borrow sentences from my books on bereavement or wo-mag platitudes. I can't connect the person that I'm talking about with the self who used to have actual feelings. Who used to have a daughter. I can't connect. Will the rest of my life be played out in the past tense – a constant future retrospective?

I have painted my nails with Georgina's sparkling pink nail polish. Barry-M. It is streetwise, pretty, edgy. It doesn't suit me. These hands don't belong to me. Everything that was once attached whizzes away, like a bad trip. It's like a waking nightmare. Excuse the clichés. I feel as though I'm on a space walk and the cord can't be trusted to tether me. I'm about to spin off into the blackness, never to feel anything solid beneath my feet or in my hands, ever again.

This isn't what people want to hear, when they ask how I'm doing. It's nice of them to ask:

they don't have to. I'm doing okay, all things considered.

Wednesday, 11th December 2013.

Helen Anderson posted:
Spent an emotional (in a good way!) morning hearing Georgina's music being played, and adding dedications to the Teesside Hospice Tree of Life, at the Cleveland Centre, Middlesbrough x

Saturday, 14th December 2013.

Helen Anderson posted:
Having a quiet night in after yesterday's successful Elvis tribute event at Marske Working Men's Club. Wasn't sure if I was up to going, but I'm glad I did as the atmosphere was amazing, lots more money was raised for The Teenage Cancer Trust and The Sick Children's Trust, and they played Georgina's song to a packed room xxxxx

Sunday, 15th December 2013.

Writing in pen, today. I could go all the way downstairs to get a pencil out of my handbag, but this pen is calling to me from the jumble on the top of the chest of drawers in my bedroom. Our bedroom. How does it feel different to scribble in ink, rather than graphite? The plastic outer casing is roughly the same - I use mechanical pencils – but the nib drags. The pen is heavy and it makes my hand ache, when I grip it. The Pain. It makes me wish that I had learned to hold my writing instruments correctly, rather than being stuck with my five-year-old self's haphazard fist-shape.

The pen digs deeper into the page and permeates the fibres. The words can't be altered, without the whole world knowing, so I proceed more cautiously. It slows down the connection from mind to hand by a fraction which gives me space to consider which mark to make on the world. It is impossible to sketch when you have committed yourself to ink. It feels like a big step. This pen in my hand feels powerful. It is a responsibility. It slips over the page, joining things up wherever it can.

My five-year-old fist wants to print. Unambiguous, individual letters, without flicks or loops or decoration. My five-year-old fist is quite particular about the exact proportions and relationship of each ball, stick, dot and dash. I remember the teacher trying to adjust my grip. How she sulked when my handwriting won prizes. Gothic. Italic. I can still turn on the style when I want to. I have been known to bring meetings and workshops to a halt as my neighbour makes comment on my beautiful handwriting, covering her own doodles. Such a contrast with the scrawl – the poor spelling, even - that spews forth from me in private. Such shame in what I lapse into, when nobody's looking.

Monday, 16th December 2013.

Helen Anderson posted:
Managed to conquer my technophobia and downloaded G's song multiple times on iTunes by signing in and out and manually entering

username and password each time I bought it. Go, me!!

Tuesday, 17th December 2013.

Feeling the tension rise. I can put the sandbags out but I know there will be breaches. There will be sludge – slime on the soft furnishings. I can swish the effluent away with a broom but there's nowhere for it to go. The drains weren't designed to cope with this.

We have given a radio interview to the reporter who came to speak to Georgina in hospital about her video going viral. She remembered my daughter. It was good to talk to someone who remembered her half-alive. I worry that people might think I'm enjoying the media attention. I spew out the sanitised version of Georgina's story and it is not untrue. But the more I wash the words, the more stubbornly the baked-on dirt clings to the fibres. As if the story is getting grubbier and more terrible with each rinse.

My mind's image of Georgina is like a pop-art print, becoming less distinct with each press. It is still recognisable, and, when I squint at it through half-closed eyes, it brings it back into focus. All the detail is only clear if I look away from it. It's best to step back, where I can't see the brush strokes and the individual bristles stuck in the acrylic. Where you can't see the discrepancy between the original and the reproduction.

Wednesday, 18th December 2013.

Helen Anderson posted:
Pleased to have my wonderful son home.

Helen Anderson posted:
Bydales teacher, Ms Bell, plans to swim the Channel, in memory of Georgina. Sorry to see her leaving the school.

Saturday, 21st December 2013.

Helen Anderson posted:
Thanks to everyone who has helped with Georgina's song. We will let you know how much we have raised ASAP. Now, enjoy Christmas! Xxxx

Wednesday, 25th December 2013.

Paul Anderson posted:
Helen and I wanted to say a massive thank you to everyone who has supported us through this difficult period. The 'community' feeling we have experienced from far and wide has been incredible. Have a good Christmas xx

Wednesday, 25th December 2013.

Christmas in Madeira. South coast. Funchal. Old Town. The heat is gentle and containing. The 'otherness' of this Christmas is fitting for a year which has been so horribly surprising. I have lost all points of reference. I am so lost on this floating garden island that even Henry the Navigator couldn't help me. The church bells provide temporal orientation – their different chimes are a code which the locals seem to understand, as they walk to and from the white-plastered building in groups of various sizes. I am deaf to any celebratory tone. Sounds do not necessarily equal music.

I wish I had the weight of Georgina in my lap again. Wriggling and writhing and chubby. Or cuddly and peaceful and slim. I remember the weight of her cooling hand as it stiffened around mine and the weight of her ashes as I cradled the rose-pink cardboard scatter-tube - purpose-made for dispensing my daughter - into which they had poured her.

As her dad and her brother and I sat on the bench overlooking the fishing boats near our home, waiting for an uncooperative sky to bleach itself pink, I didn't want to move. Just as I didn't want to get out of that borrowed hospital bed, squashed into my writing room on the ground floor of our home, even though I was only held in by side rails locked into position by the Macmillan nurse. I could have lain there all night, watching her chest not rising and not falling. I had cramp in my arm, but I did not want to leave her alone to let the air leech the lost drops of humanity out of her. The nurse let the side rails down and persuaded me to help her wash Georgina's body. We changed her pyjamas and covered her head with the pink scarf which we had come to associate with her.

When the funeral directors came, there was a practised expression of sadness on their faces. I suppose it was genuine. They wore formal suits, even though it was the middle of the night. The doctor who had been called didn't know the English system for dealing with the dead and took the nurse's word as to which forms needed to be signed. She lightly brushed a finger against Georgina's neck and confirmed that there was nothing.

"Bless her", she said, and filled out the paperwork. I remember – or I might be imagining - how her crystal crucifix pendant caught the light of the candles I had lit. Candles, everywhere, now, as if an eternal flame might keep Georgina – and the rest of us – alive. Woodberry, Clean Linen, Sandalwood and Vanilla, all burning together. Normal rules don't apply at such times.

By the boats, the sky didn't turn pink, but rays of sun rose through the morning's grey clouds like an art deco stained glass door panel, and we knew that it was time. We took it in turns to scatter her. The wind wasn't quite strong enough to carry her out to sea. Chalky powder fell onto wet golden mud. There were granules and the odd chunk that I fancied were bone from lithe limbs. They might have been pieces of coffin, or fragments of her new slippers. I don't suppose they separate it all out. I don't suppose that it can or should be sifted.

I scattered her, unidentified bits and all. I inadvertently took some of my daughter home in the turn-ups of my jeans, shaking out the grains of her as we walked the dog back up our street, where people were waking. I found bits of her in unlikely places, later – like confetti in a bride's corset.

Last night, according to Paul, I was singing "Silent Night" in my sleep.

<u>Sunday, 29th December 2013.</u>

In a café clinging to the cliff over the bay of Funchal. Below, the tourists load off cruise ships, wearing a hotchpotch of uncertain, Winter Sun outfits; white trousers, black fleeces, tropical print t-shirts. They peel off and pile on layers. They are prepared for any eventuality, but they never quite look correctly clad.

I used to be afraid of heights but I am perched up here with the gulls. I eat chocolate cake with almonds and red fruit that we think might be cranberries. Cranberries interfere with Paul's medication. I press into the fruit glaze with the sharp edge of my cake fork and lift crumbs to my mouth in between gusts of Atlantic wind. The sweetness doesn't match the bitter aftertaste of my 'bica' – the local, black-black coffee concentrated into an unfeasibly small cup made of coarse, white china.

I am perched on this terrace, carved just above the waterline. The iron balustrade will stop me from falling. It wasn't the actual height that I used to be afraid of – it was the falling. Somehow, the falling holds no fear for me now. If I fall, I fall. The seagulls watch me with cranberry-red eyes, poised to scavenge on my bones. Tomorrow, we will fly home, and I will be suspended higher still, and then dropped back down into a strange, changed home.

Tuesday, 31st December 2013.

Helen Anderson posted:
Catching up on the Marske Boxing Day Dip pictures. So many people took part in memory of Georgina, including the lovely Amber, sporting a v cool t-shirt! Well done!! Community spirit in action for my girl on Boxing Day xxxxx Thanks to everyone who dipped and 'sorry' I couldn't join you because I was basking in the Madeiran sun!!

Tuesday, 31st December 2013.

Back from Madeira. We came home to a Christmas card from an old university friend who I must have forgotten to tell about Georgina. She includes Georgina's name in it. She hopes that we are all well. I know she'll feel terrible when I tell her.

Ignoring Christmas worked well for me, and I would try the same tactic for New Year, but my husband won't play ball. He's gone to the pub with his best mate, who is known in our household as 'Big Paul', to differentiate him from my (slightly smaller) husband. This is his way of ignoring New Year, too. I am alone with my thoughts and with this past year's diary. The diary is split into two: before and after Diagnosis Day. 18th July, 2013, when nothing was the same again.

On New Year's Eve, I have a tradition of transferring recurring key dates from this year into next. Dates like birthdays – usually pretty much the same, year on year. This year, it's as if someone's stuck a big fat thumb in the metronome and bent the ticker. Then, they've tried to set it going again so that nobody will notice, but it lurches out of time in the middle of key pieces. I might try to bring it back to the centre, but it's never quite at rest. There's always the suggestion of a tremble, especially if I stare at it. It wiggles like a time-shift in a movie. Flashback. Colour to sepia. Flash forward, but when the shimmering stops and I wake up, I do not find that it was all a dream.

My son is at home. He has stayed in with me this evening. I feel that he is guarding me. He knows how deep into despair I can descend, and he doesn't trust the shiny, coping new me. He clomps around the house, dyspraxic. Trying to fill all the spaces left empty by his little sister. He fills them with his thuds and sighs and stout limbs and encyclopaedic knowledge of parliamentary protocol and his various other specialist subjects. He has devised a numeric code for various emotions he can't quite express.

"I was a bit 878-ish, earlier, but now I've had a word with myself and things are a lot 243-er".

It is funny – but not funny – how unlike my daughter my son is. He is alive, for one thing (not funny). He lets me cuddle him. I hold his feet, remembering to apply pressure to the balls of his feet, which is his preference. My daughter, too, liked a foot massage (it is funny how they are/were alike) but she preferred me to wiggle each toe, individually. I stroke his head, which sprouts copper and gold. He has a double crown, which looks like a weird fingerprint. A whorl, perhaps. I used to know the names for different finger-skin patterns.

Fingerprints were one of the things we were taught at school. Like the Shapes of Leaves – sycamore; oak; chestnut; the obvious ones, as well as the obscure ones and the ones you should never touch. We were taught UK Birds; the names of the Three Kings and their respective gifts; Why We Have Fireworks, and Roman Place-Names. We were taught Primary Colours and Which Colours Mix Together to Make Which Other Colours. But nobody could tell me where the primary colours came from, in the first place. No, they wouldn't answer that.

My son smells of aftershave. He smells of shower gel For Men, which reminds me that my sniffing behind his ears is no longer entirely appropriate behaviour, even though he may tolerate it. I have let go of my son once, when he went to university, and even if I try to reel him in again now, the cord between us doesn't quite snap back. It sags, rather than coiling up between us. I will have to slacken my grip on him again, come the start of the new term. My son stays at home, tonight, guarding me, although he says he's researching his essay on the internet. His dissertation? I should know what his dissertation is about.

I flick through the past year, daring myself to remember it. I sneck it shut and light another candle. A candle, now, in every corner of this too-many-bedroomed, too-detached house.

Wednesday, 1st January 2014.

Helen Anderson posted:
Last year taught me many lessons, including that we never know what's round the corner, so we need to make the most of what we've got right now xxx (profound)

Thursday, 2nd January 2014.

It's the second day of a writing challenge I came across on Facebook. I have signed up to it, via a proper website, and paid for daily prompts. They have been duly received, and yesterday I wrote:

Red roses in a jam jar
Forced too soon for Valentine's Day
Positioned in the hearth in place of coals.

I think it might be a poem, or the beginnings of one. I gazed around my lounge for a long time, to come up with that. I don't seem to produce the same kind of poetic imagery as the other writers posting on the blog. They seem so tuned in to Nature, but all that moss and lichen and peat and granite and brine makes me itch. It is not my natural habitat, and I don't trust it, especially now.

I am a centrally-heated, cavity-wall insulated, breeze block, Formica kind of girl. I can see the character of character homes – the charm of their original features. But wall-to-wall carpeting and fitted wardrobes and secondary double-glazing were the features of my childhood, and I am not going to claim a less suburban heritage, purely for the sake of my lit-cred. I am rooted in porcelain, thatched cottage-shaped, souvenir lamps. Mine was a childhood of crazy-paved drives and wallflower and nasturtium borders. My diet was of Angel Delight and pop and deliveries by van from the frozen food shop, stashed in the chest freezer in the garage.

Though I broke out via university and years abroad and jobs in London, I came back to it. This extended Sixties house in an overgrown village not quite next to the North Sea is my reference point. This avenue which used to be lined with trees which the neighbours are chopping down just as they're maturing because they're so afraid of what the roots might do to their foundations.

Friday, 3rd January 2014.

I meet a mental health nurse, to 'offload'. I talk about the spare seat at the dining table and about finding out who your real friends are when times are tough. I talk in clichés, but they feel authentic. The nurse thinks I have been avoiding talking about my feelings. I have been avoiding feeling my feelings.

I tried to write this earlier today, but I found other calls on my time and energy. I chose to spend time with my son, instead. Avoidance, perhaps, but I don't want to regret putting my writing before my remaining child, if there is a chance that he wants me. I am tired of regretting. I never want to have another regret, ever again. I realise that is an impossibility, as soon as I write that sentence. Nonsense-talk. Bottom-speak.

This evening, we were invited to Big Paul's house for a curry. Big Paul is guarding us, too, but he created a small gathering, to make it less obvious. There were two ladies (I include myself in this number) and five gents present. The conversation quickly turned to football. I am astounded at the menfolk's ability to record and recall the fine detail of football matches. League table movements. Past and future fixtures. Timings of goals.

I am tempted to scoff at the seriousness with which they regurgitated the minutiae, challenging each other to recount – with painful clarity - incidents which may or may not have taken place. They reached a place where it doesn't matter if it was 2-1 or 2-0 at half-time. Where it does matter, but their comradeship matters more. And anyway, each and every gent is certain that he is the only one remembering correctly. I am tempted to mock, but I envy their certainty and their ability to bring to mind exact shades that were only ever imagined.

I lose myself in the liveliness of their discussion – in the passion with which they repeat lines from old films and replayed slapstick scenes. They retell the same old stories – lightly tweaked – and the listeners hang onto each word so convincingly that I wonder if their evident anticipation of the punchline might be genuine. It's as if they have all signed up to a dementia pact, so that the tales can be told again. Collective amnesia. Yet, they all know exactly when to laugh, and there is real happiness in that laughter. The happiness of knowing the script and playing your part. I wish that I didn't have this urge to ad-lib and disrupt the show.

They deliver joke after in-joke to appreciative faces. They sing theme tunes and name titles of episodes. I am in no position to join in or contradict. I wondered what I was doing there. It reminded me of staying at a relative's house, where there's no time off from the small talk. Where it's rude to sleep in late, because they've set the breakfast table properly, with juice and fruit and a cafetiere, even though it's normally *Sugar Puffs* in front of the TV. Where you interpret the clicks of the bathroom door, to work out when it's okay to sneak in and have your shower without holding up the whole household and throwing them off-schedule. That feeling of being a nuisance, even though you're aiming to be no-trouble-at-all, as the kids who've been made to give up their bedrooms give voice to the question that everyone's choking back.

"How long are you here for?"

When are you going home?

Where you can't wait to get back home, but you can't get comfy there, either. That homesickness. This desperation to sign back up with the devil you know.

Sunday, 5th January 2014.

I have moved my desk back into the 'garden room', which won't actually be my 'writing room' again until I've put pen or pencil to paper – or fingertips to computer keys for purposes other than social media – in there. It still has an air of being the 'room where Georgina died'. The Dying Room.

When I sit at my desk again, I'll be in the exact spot where she lay, those last two weeks, in her bed. Where I lay next to her on her last night, for as long as it was going to take. Except that Georgina was not facing the wall, as I will be, but facing her dad, who was crouched on a footstool next to the patio doors. For as long as it was going to take, as her eyes lost focus and she grunted slowly and exquisitely, he held her hand and I 'spooned' her. How she would have hated me to use that expression.

The cot side held me in and dug into my flank and turned me numb, as we tried to find our daughter's special place. A place special enough for her to spend the rest of eternity. Her place was in the city. New York. Times Square. Bright lights and skyscrapers. Cruising in a yellow cab on the set of a film. I felt like I was in a film. I couldn't pinpoint the exact moment when life left Georgina. It was more of a gradual emptying. I could only say that she was definitely gone, in retrospect.

There has been a lot of retrospection, recently, but only the first bubblings of tears. I can just about look back on things and events, but I can't look at myself. Not yet. I know that there is more, just out of view. I try to look forward, but I can't go there. Not yet.

I feel as if I've reached the second level of the Eiffel Tower, and this is quite something, given my lifelong terror of heights. I want to say "To hell with it, I might as well go right to the top!" but, instead, I crawl back into the lift and press

'Down'. I crawl back there on my knees because I can't bear the wind biting at the mesh which has been put there to save people like me. It looks a bit on the flimsy side. And I don't even trust the lift, but I prefer its glass sides to the open staircase spiralling downwards, like a nightmare zooming in and out. There is the inevitable loss of footing. When I'm back on terra firma, I might laugh from relief – or so that people will be laughing with me, rather than at me – but I'll be steering well clear of Paris, in future.

I might brush up on my Dutch. The language of flatness. I wonder if Lanzarote is still sticking to its low-rise planning regulations. I might go back to Lanzarote.

I cannot go back into that room, which does not have an official function. I need to write, in that room, at my desk – surrounded by my own things and by my daughter's. I need to make it a new space, connected to – but not stuck in – the past. In particular, it must not be stuck in those terrible, living-dead days. I need to put the heating on and light candles and play not-too-happy-not-too-sad music, in there, and see what happens

Monday, 6th January 2014.

Strictly speaking – and I do like to speak strictly – it is Tuesday, already forty minutes old.

The dog is not well. He heaves when he eats. He snores with every breath, though he's not even sleeping. We are taking him to the vets in the morning, if things don't improve. It's already morning. He's only a dog but I've just let myself love him again, after farming him out to Paul's dad's for months, and cutting off from worrying about him because, in the scheme of things, he was only a dog. I don't want to hear what the vet's got to say, unless it's "Some antibiotics will soon put him right."

I went with Paul to see his cardiologist (Paul's, not the dog's) today/yesterday. His annual check-up. It's the first time he's wanted me to go to the appointment with him, for years. I don't think he could bear to tell his doctor his news, all by himself. Between us, we got it out. We filled each other's gaps. The cardiologist was kind. He asked technical questions about the cancer: its onset and its presentation. He was shaken - you can tell which doctors are parents. He let Paul tell the story and once Paul's words started, he couldn't stop. Especially about Georgina's singing and how good Middlesbrough Football Club have been. I felt sorry for picking a fight with Paul yesterday.

My husband is a broken man. He is a shadow of himself. All the clichés (some of them are good ones). The cardiologist asked about other, surviving offspring: if Joe were his son - he used the correct tense and I was glad that he wasn't too emotional to abandon grammar – he would want his aorta to be checked. Every ten years, at least. Sometimes these things look alright when they're young, but ten/twenty years on, problems manifest. Paul commented how lucky it was that our son does not have a bicuspid valve, like his father and his late sister, but the doctor's non-committal silence on the matter reminded me of Georgina's oncologist's.

Not wanting to be cruel. Not wanting to give false assurances.

"If it were my son, I'd want him to be checked."

I nodded and stressed that we'd tell him, wondering how you tell someone something like that without crippling them. When I got home, I went to the loo. By the time I came out, Paul 'casually' 'mentioned' he'd told Joe about it on the phone. So we silently agreed not to dwell on the matter. Not right now.

I worry about the dog. Maybe the snorting's just down to a cold. Maybe. He's never had a cold like this before.

Saturday, 11th January 2014.

Today, the panic came over me. It trickled from my temples and I was so hot that I had to take my scarf off and unbutton my double breasted pea coat, in the middle of Yorkshire Trading.

I'd gone into town with my son: left him manning the 'Cost of Cameron' stall in the High Street with his political pals. One of the ladies thought we'd met before. I said I didn't think so – I don't think so – but she definitely recognised my face. Perhaps from the school gates, she thought, and I didn't want to say "Perhaps from the papers. I'm the woman with the dead daughter." My legs barely carried me to the discount book shop. I bought nothing, but I did a good impression of a person who might actually be browsing. I scurried to Yorkshire Trading and I bought sugar, in the form of chocolate buttons, to stave off the faint which keeps threatening but hasn't (yet) felled me. I remember the horror; the burning, sick throat; the weak-kneed steadying as I felt the CCTV clock my nervous perspiration. I picked up a bottle of mineral water and wondered how they could sell it so cheap. I considered the dog chews section, carefully focusing on the labels because our dog's on a gluten-free, dairy-free diet. I perused the tea towels – a lady can't have too many tea towels – but couldn't choose between the checks and the chintz. Hoping for the ultimate sugar high, I added a bag of Revels to my basket. My hand picked it off the shelf, as if I had that syndrome where one, evil hand does the very things that your civilised rest-of-self would never even admit to thinking about. I remembered to pay.

I sat on a bench, outside, letting the cold air waft through the weave of my aptly-named sweater. I glugged the water down, without even checking that the seal had not been tampered with. This you-can't-hurt-me attitude – this grim, devil-may-care abandon - will be the death of me. I downed the bag of Buttons in one go. I opened the Revels and wondered if they tasted odd, or if this was just a penalty of switching straight from Cadburys to Mars, without cleansing my palate. I steamed my way to Beales department store and thought about buying a handbag. Then, I filled a wire basket with candles. Reduced. An absolute necessity. Sniffing the wax for the most meaningful scents, I looked forward to drawing the curtains and watching the flames.

I rendezvoused with my son. We had veggie burgers in the pub and I couldn't believe how full it was, at two o'clock on a sunny January Saturday. All those couples, sitting opposite each other, wordlessly daubing patterns in the grains of salt on the table tops and occasionally looking up at the horses racing silently across the flat screen. They all looked alike. If you can't tell who's won until they flash up the results, you might as well only watch right at the end.

My son and I talked about taking road trips across Australia and he showed me Amtrak timetables, on his iPhone, because America would be easier to get to. He wondered whether the health insurance costs for his father might outweigh any benefit of shorter, cheaper flights. Such spontaneity. Even my son's sense of adventure is tempered – almost snuffed out - by our middle-aged concerns. All this talk of a long-haul trip from a woman who can't walk around her hometown without being engulfed by terror. Maybe, the further away I get, the braver I will be. Maybe not: it's the risk, and risk paralyses. I draw the curtains and light the candles.

This time tomorrow, my son will be gone, too. I'll be the-woman-with-the-clever-son-in-London-and-the-dead-daughter. Or people will find me flickeringly familiar but be unable to put a story to my face. The dog is enjoying his chews, biting down with appreciation and amazement at my cleverness in knowing just what he wanted. They don't seem to be sticking in his throat or in any of his other passages. I check myself, as soon as this thought formulates, in case God is watching and planning further punishments for my pride and self-congratulation.

Tonight, I spoke on the phone to a relative who's having trouble with her children's school. I wanted to – I didn't - shout "So what? It could be worse!" like Paul did, last week, when the overworked mechanic started listing his domestic problems, by way of explanation as to why my Micra still hasn't been serviced and he hasn't been returning our calls. Paul warned him not to go there – he definitely gave him a chance to dig himself out of the hole – but still the mechanic went on about his wife's nightshifts and the staff sickness rates and the management's unrealistic expectations until Paul trumped him with a fifteen-year old girl's death. That was the end of the matter, after the apologies and the back-tracking and the offers of speedy, discounted attention. But what if the mechanic had said "So what?" back to Paul? What then? I let my relative list her problems. People still have lives.

I wonder if it is exploitative to write about Georgina. Or, at least, sensationalist or sentimental. The last thing I want is to use her. But it's not about gaining sympathy. It's not about creating a stir or a name for myself. Right now, it's about having an outlet for my grief. I hope that writing these thoughts down will help me to process and contain it. I want to write. I need, need, need to write. One day, I might use these words to shape another book, or I might send them out into the world, raw. One day, in some way, I plan to use this diary to bear witness to the disaster which has befallen our girl and us.

Saturday, 11th January 2014.

The furniture in my Writing Room is constantly on the move. I have decided to put things back in an entirely different layout, because the original is impossible to recreate. Even if I used the same nail-holes in the walls and the dents in the carpet-pile as a guide, it could never be the same as before. This is now, and that was then. I leave some of her pictures and her fairy lights in place. They are sustaining, even though I can barely bring myself to look at them.

Tuesday, 14th January 2014.

A quick one, because I need to go to bed. My eyes are watering with tiredness, or maybe with something worse given that it's two months today since my daughter died and all her friends are posting on Facebook about her. All beautiful, terrible statuses. I've got 'hay fever' which the medication's not quite touching. I've got an ache in my belly, where Georgina once was. This is a peculiar strain of hay fever. Most peculiar. It seems to be catching, because Facebook is awash with streaming eyes. Maybe I should eschew modern medicine and go for a natural remedy. Maybe I should go homeopathic and keep administering a miniscule dose of my daughter to myself, until she cures me. Maybe I should accept that I'll always suffer with this.

Wednesday, 15th January 2014.

Walking home from the village shops, I bumped into a girl from Georgina's year. She stopped and talked, even though she didn't know what to say. Then, I bumped into a girl from the year below, who stopped and talked, too. We talked about her little sister's trip to the dentist, and I told her little sister (whose name I have already forgotten) that it would soon be over and done with.

I did not bump into Georgina, though quite a few of the girls coming out of school have her pre-chemo hairstyle. Their clothing is uniform, whether they are in schoolwear, or not. A few have her skinny legs, but their knees don't knock like goose-knees. They don't roll in on one foot. No-one has my girl's walk. I tried on her shoes but they didn't fit. I don't know if I could have walked a few steps in Georgina's shoes – never mind mile-after-mile for four solid, quagmire months.

I don't know how my daughter didn't cry. I wonder if that's why she didn't want to be left alone. Being brave for others keeps you sane for yourself. We're all still colluding: Stay Strong! If one link weakens, the whole thing will fall down and it wouldn't be pretty. It's not pretty, anyway, but at least we're all safe and dry. High and dry, rather than low and wet. Things get dangerous when wet.

I don't know how she faced the truth, head-on. She stared it down, whereas I can glance at it for a split second, then my corneas sizzle. She saved her corneas, so that there was some of her left over for others. Living on. I wonder what her transplanted corneas see. I wonder if there'll be anything left of me, undamaged enough to donate. I glance at it; make contact; sweep sideways. I fix on the floor, where I have to place my feet, one in front of the other. I am like a child jiggling to stop herself from having an accident. Skiddy. Slippery, like the truth.

When I got home, I sat in the Writing Room. I cried, but I didn't stay there long. Five minutes, perhaps – long enough, given the chill radiating through the floor. Long enough, given my stockinged feet. I feel like none of my own shoes even fit. They all rub and pinch – each with a different type of meanness. I can just about bear the pressure of my socks. Extra-comfort. I snapped them up in Tesco.

Tonight, we're going to Cineworld to see the new film about Nelson Mandela. Maybe I'll be able to cry if I lose myself in a different sorrow. What kind of mother doesn't cry, when her own daughter's body disintegrates, right next to her? But I did cry, then. I am almost forgetting that I did cry: it was in organising the funeral that I switched off the stopcock, for practical reasons. And now I can't find it again, so I pretend there was never water at all. Like living in a strange house that's all plumbed in but where the pipes lead nowhere.

This house I'm living in is dark. Candles help, but I daren't leave them on for long. The burning worries me: if you turn your back for a second, the whole thing could go up in smoke. In a single second, everything could be gone. Crisped to perfection. Obliterated.

Friday, 24th January 2014.

A whirl of a week. I feel sick, dizzy, thrilled. I am so happy and so miserable. The school held a memorial day. It was called G-Day but there is a new head teacher who didn't know my daughter and the planned events were scaled down. They are having a drive on discipline, and the children were lectured on their behaviour in front of us, which I didn't think was necessary. When it was time for my speech, I had their full attention. I told my version of Georgina's story. I had my say. I claimed it. I talked about crying. I told them it was okay to cry and I've never felt so calm in all of my life. At last, when the new head had finished, I had a chance to talk directly to her friends and her teachers, with no need to put a spin on anything.

When the reporters came, later, to take photos of the kids with the Middlesbrough Football Club chef and the Boro footballers and the world champion female boxer who'd all come in to inspire the young people about their futures, I lost my words. They deserted me. They went scurrying back below my voice box (that may not be how it all works, technically, but that's how it felt) like Nurofen, swallowed dry, on an empty stomach.

A delegation of Georgina's girlfriends came to find me in the school staff room, at lunch break. We stood on the landing and chatted about nothing. Nothing has never felt so wonderful (the double-negative being totally intentional). Their giggles and their banter felt like the warmest, bravest embrace. I asked them for a cuddle.

Georgina's friend, Amber, still doesn't like cuddles, but I do, now, when I can get them. She obliged. The bell rang for afternoon school – more of a siren – and I wanted to make them late for class. Their fashions are changing already. Soon, I won't know about the correct style of school shoes or school bag. I won't know whether partings are being worn at the side or the centre and whether curly or straight is in. Already, I feel so out of touch, in so many ways.

When I got home, I crawled under my blanket on the sofa, but a man called round about my Nissan Micra. Last week, I wanted to sell it, but today I didn't. Not yet. I resisted the urge to talk him out of buying it. No more Mum's Taxi-trips for that Micra, anyway. No more flipping the front seat forward to fit in Amber and her sleepover prerequisites in the back. It would have felt old and useless, in any case. It was kinder to let that old car go, but I still miss it already. Even though it was time, I feel guilty. It would never have been a good time. They picked it up while I was at therapy.

I went to the petrol station, solely to buy a bottle of white wine. I took the dog: bought a magazine and bag of pasta, as cover. I was wearing my wellies – hulking great treads on the soles, but still I lost my footing on ice. Black ice and white ice. I cried my way along the street in the dark, dodging the security lights that I triggered as I passed. I was so afraid of falling, like last year, when I slipped and broke my arm. Last year, I thought my life was coming together. Pride. Falls. Et cetera.

On Tuesday, I wanted to blame Paul. For everything. I wanted to blame him for the furore surrounding Georgina's friend, Mia's head-shave and her school's disapproval of it. I wanted to blame him for the hour spent sitting in the car outside the house of the man who was framing the donated football shirt for the charity do, at cost price. I wanted to blame Paul because the café had run out of jacket potatoes and I always have a jacket potato. I couldn't admit that the replacement panini was actually okay. Such a fuss. Later, when we decided to find it all funny, I blamed hunger.

There was a fundraising concert in memory of Georgina at the neighbouring school. We were guests of honour. The kids' faces were filled with the pleasure of knowing they were doing a good thing, mixed with fear at getting up and singing in front of their peers. They jiggled and they twiddled with their jewellery. They got the giggles. Some of them went off-key but it didn't grate. It didn't matter, because they were singing for Georgina, even if they'd never sung before. Paul gave a lovely speech and everyone cried. Everyone – except me. I felt happy – I ached with it.

Tonight, we're going on a coach to a fundraising concert starring *X Factor's* Abi Alton. I hope that none of the kids are ill on the coach. Suddenly, it feels like every child in the world is my responsibility. It's as if I need to save as many as I can. I have sorted my outfit for the outing. I have exhausted my supply of Georgina-trademark pink clothes, but I have a bright fuchsia satchel. I need to do my nails but I don't know what colours and finish are in fashion. I trawl through magazines, hoping that some of the instructions on What Not to Wear will inspire. There's nobody else to ask. I need to trust my own judgement, but I trust that least of all. It's at times like these that I need my daughter. I need my daughter at lots of times – like these, and not like these.

Saturday, 25th January 2014.

Helen Anderson posted:
Shattered after a busy week packed with events in memory of G. But it's a 'good' type of 'shattered' as I'm proud that so many people want to honour her xxxxx

Sunday, 26th January 2014.

Tears today. I went to Middlesbrough with my friend Caytie and her daughter Amelia. Georgina's childhood friend, Holly, and Amelia were having a get-together to talk about Georgina and old times. I listened to their banter in the back of the car. Their witticisms made me ache. I wanted to be near these girls and I wanted to be as far away from them as possible. The way Caytie and Amelia tease each other reminded me of Georgina and me. Georgina may have been taken, but I had the pleasure of having her as my daughter. I am still her mum, and that will never change.

I told Caytie that I'd had a good time and I was okay, but when I got home my false brightness was choking me. I sat in that room where she died and felt the coldness of the tiled floor creep into me. I looked up to the skylight that Georgina could see from her deathbed. My mouth filled with acid and I held it there a while. Then, I swallowed. I climbed under the blanket crocheted for me by my sister. The holes in the pattern let cold air in, but I had nothing else.

Tuesday, 28th January 2014.

Chloe has posted photos of herself and Georgina on Facebook, commenting that they look identical. There is indeed a likeness, apart from the hated tube taped to Georgina's face. It was the day Georgina had shaved off her hair, which was barely clinging on. She put on her new, 'real' wig. Chloe styled it for her and helped her put make-up on. They both have exquisite almond eyes, lined with deep kohl and defined with sooty lashes. They pout for the selfie.

The social worker from the hospital visited today. It has stirred up memories of that ward, with its purple-striped décor and the glitter on the bathroom floor. It has stirred up memories of the bleeping machines, and of the puking, and of cups of tea from the water-heater which never quite boiled. I think about the oncologists with whom I've shared the worst, most intimate moments of my life. I long to meet them again, and I dread it. I want them to tell me that I'm not crazy – that this happened. Yet, I'd prefer to be certified crazy – to be told that this is one long psychotic episode. Then I could take their pills and wait for sanity to set back in.

Saturday, 1st February 2014.

Chloe's sixteenth birthday. I put a card containing some money through her letterbox. I fretted that it wasn't the right house, even though I've dropped her home there at least ten times.

My forty-sixth birthday has now passed. It passed pleasantly and without untoward incident. Paul bought me a new Nissan Micra, as a surprise. It was sweet of him to go all the way to Sheffield to pick it up. I didn't know he was gone. It was sweet of him to go all that way to try to lift me out of the doldrums. Joe sent me a new coffee machine – such a typically 'Joe' gift. Practical but thoughtful. For Joe, a caffeine supply is a top priority and he worries I'm not getting enough. Oh, and I got flowers and notebooks and pens. Paul gave me a vintage suitcase. It is dented and lined with checked paper. There are no keys to the locks but it will hold my papers. It will contain my words for me, until they are ready.

I was given wine. Georgina's friend Callum and his Mum, Jan, who I've not previously met, turned up on my doorstep with a bottle of champagne and brave smiles. It was painful to be near a close friend of Georgina's. How do they all bear sitting alongside each other every day, in school, knowing that Georgina is missing? It must be hard. The surprise visit was a joy and a pleasure, and left me aching as Callum's school uniform left the porch.

We spent my birthday evening at a Greek taverna, discussing the possibility of an early summer holiday. We can't recreate those early, past summers, but they say the off-season can be nice, if you don't expect perfection. Paul and I talked and I tried to be transported in space and time by grilled aubergines and pungent Feta and giant butter beans. There was dry, dry wine, dripping from a tin jug. We drank thick, Greek coffee, and I was not woman enough to swallow the grinds at the bottom. Do they watch from the kitchen and laugh at our attempts to gulp it, with a weak Nescafé at the ready? The simplicity of the blue and white décor – the limited palette – soothed me.

The roses. I am so spoilt that I forgot to mention the red roses that Paul gave me. My husband has tried to think of everything. They were hand-tied, with waxy green foliage bound by raffia.

And the cards, mainly turquoise and pink, this year. I know how hard they must have been to write. How tricky it must have been to find the right wording. How many were reconsidered; scrunched-up, and binned? I appreciate all the effort that has gone into not offending me. All the time taken to find the right tone. Even where the tone jars and jangles, I appreciate the effort and time.

Last night, I went out for a meal with friends I hadn't seen for a while, and they held me gently. They knew I wouldn't want hugging. They held me with their quiet concern and the lilt of their conversation. They presented me with birthday chocolates, when the coffees were brought out. We dived straight in. They shooed me home, while they worked out the intricacies of the bill. My knees barely made it home. I cuddled into Paul and we watched an old episode of *Prime Suspect*.

94

I texted my friend to say I wouldn't be driving to Scarborough to a writing workshop. I knew it was too much of an undertaking, but I had wanted to push myself. But there is pushing oneself, and there is self-annihilation. I went to bed relieved. I slept in, for the first time in weeks. I'm told I was snoring worse than usual. Paul brought me tea and ginger jam on toast and I stayed in that messy bed in that pigsty bedroom until three in the afternoon. I ran a bath. I bathed in the extra-mild 2-in-1 Baby Bubbles and Wash that we bought for Georgina. Now, I have to do things for both us – live two lives in one. She was just moving on to Hollister shower gel and shampoo for over-treated hair. She was dousing herself in Rihanna's new perfume and eying up my Dr Hauschka oils. Then, she was plunged straight back into baby bath – the safest option for sick skin. No more tears, it said. Unfragranced, it says. But nothing smells of nothing.

Monday, 3rd February 2014.

I've taken to my bed. For three consecutive days, now, I've got up and tried to be normal and my head has rung and I have felt sick and I've ached. I am hot and I am cold. I tried to ignore it. I told myself it was all in my head. Finally, I realised that it may have started in my head, but this sickness is real in my pelvis; my back; my legs. I am taking it as a warning, no matter whether it's physical or psychological. I have been forced to slow down, if not yet brought to a total stop. The warning lights are flashing bright and orange. It would be madness to set out in a blizzard, knowing that there is a fault.

Then, I think of Georgina's pain and suffering. I think how glad she would have been to have woken up one morning and felt only as ill as I do now. I feel so ashamed – my nausea is nothing, in comparison. She probably – definitely - felt worse than this, when she last went into school. I feel useless and old, but feeling like this is also self-indulgence. I am wallowing, and not once did Georgina wallow. She may have snapped and she may have fought, but she did not give in to misery. She was not wallowing in misery, even hours before she died, when she said "I hate this" and the Macmillan nurse and the social worker confirmed that that was what her slurred sounds meant. Georgina only said it once.

It's hard to live up to that kind of courage. After three days of some stupid old virus, I am weepy and hopeless. I want my mum, but the last thing I want is my mum. It's only flu. Probably. I can ride this out. This is what my sensible head tells me. If only I had put on my sensible head, today.

Tuesday, 4th February 2014.

I got up. The nausea is less threatening – lower-seated in my gut. I am wearing loungewear, so I'm not committed to answering the door or going outside, but, then again, I could if the whim takes me. I am almost decent, except for the unwashed hair. It would be my hair which would shock people the most, if they saw it how it really is – dry, oily, kinking, muted tawny. Trying to

96

creep back into its natural dog-leg, off-centre parting.

Today, a friend of mine texted me to tell me he has cancer. Thyroid, which is a 'good' cancer to get, in that it's largely slow-growing and is capable of being cured. They are as confident as they can be that they have got it. They'll administer radio-iodine after further tests, to maximise his chances. He has known about his cancer since September and had surgery in December. If this were Georgina's cancer, he would already be dead.

I tell my friend that I'm shocked and I thank him for trying to spare my feelings, although I don't expect the whole world to stop just because my world has stopped. I don't expect people to stop getting cancer. We are going to meet, next week, for a cup of tea. I hope I don't go and upset him by mentioning death.

<u>Thursday, 6th February 2014.</u>

I almost crashed. I was concentrating too hard on concentrating and I didn't see the car creeping up on my inside. I was in my new car – all shiny and up-to-date. It nearly got a very big dent in it, after a week on the road. I was going too slowly in the fast lane and he got impatient. I think he enjoyed beeping his horn and shaking his head melodramatically. I swerved – avoided the crash. For now, at least. I've parked in Tesco car park. It's twenty minutes' drive from home and that feels like a long way. I need plates saying "Dead Daughter". Even then, I'm not sure that the other drivers would know how much space I need.

Best to keep your distance – to give me a wide berth. I'm having a coffee, to wake me up. It's a fine balance, getting my nerves out of bed on the right side.

I need Georgina. I need her to come in from school, bringing a draught in on the tails of her blazer and complaining about this or that teacher or an obnoxious Year 7. I need to talk to her about fashion and make-up and tolerance and being a person of your word. I need to find a place to be with her. Maybe I'll go down by the boats but she might not be there. I might not find her, and what then?

I saw my daughter's Death Certificate, today. It was crazy to see her date of birth, followed by her date of death. Filled in already, when it should still be a blank. A dash. An asterisk.

<u>Wednesday, 12th February 2014.</u>

Paul is burning some of Georgina's tracks onto a CD, to be played at a Valentine's Day charity event. I have been picking which tracks to include, given the limited space. I end up saying "I'm not keen on 'With or Without You'" and I feel like I'm betraying Georgina – like I'm saying she's no good. But I'm not saying she's not good: it's just not a good recording, with its background hiss. And the guitar anthem backing track keeps barging centre-stage – trying to steal her limelight, while Georgina lets her voice speak for itself. She didn't believe in showy, scene-stealing tactics. She believed in honest song.

I select five tracks which I hope show her in a way that she wouldn't dislike, but it's like choosing her a Christmas present: the need to get it perfect; to delight her; to be a top mum. The terror of misjudging it slightly but awfully. Are there degrees to which you can get this kind of thing wrong? Would 'Wherever You Will Go' be less wrong? I don't want to package her up in an out-of-date outfit, like a Stage Mum who doesn't know she's not quite down-with-the-kids.

I hear Georgina's voice singing out from the Mac propped on the kitchen table. That table is covered with an oil-cloth bought to protect it from splashes as we measured out Georgina's palliative medicines. There's a crack in her voice, which she closes just when you think that the note might develop a chink. It is the voice of a glorious woman-child. Paused. Holding a single, true note forever.

Thursday, 13th February 2014.

My mouth is healing, where the kind student dentists in Newcastle kindly dug out my rotten root. I no longer have a dry socket: a membrane is stretching over the gap. My tongue-tip finds its way there, over and over. It is healing well, but some foods catch on the newly-grown tissue. I'm not quite up to a normal, solid diet, just yet.

Tuesday, 18th February 2014.

A few days in Northumberland. Today, we went to The Alnwick Garden. I don't think that Georgina would have liked it. It was a nice place, but she wasn't one for greenery. The city – that was Georgina's place. London. New York. The glint of marble, glass and steel.

I enjoyed the quiet, contemplating the water features under the Spring-like sky. Sunlight in February is no more the order of things than snow in August. Snowdrops were pushing through, with leggy, chive stems and trembling swan necks. They reminded me of Georgina, shivering in a party dress. In the shop, they sold daffodils sprouting in terracotta pots. I couldn't see snowdrops anywhere, except in the ground, all around me. None to take home.

Friday, 21st February 2014.

We have spent the week in wellies and layers of clothing dug out from the squashed end of my wardrobe. I have revelled in the lack of glamour, though I am still wearing BB cream and 'nude', long-lasting lip tint. Nobody knows me here. The people we have met know as much as they need to. Maybe what they see is all that I am. Maybe it's that easy to walk away from yourself. I've been doing a lot of walking here – jarring steps on uneven ground. My sciatic nerve is in shock. The mud has been collecting in the treads of my virgin, black wellies as I roll along the country lanes, trying to keep my grip.

We have discovered Barter Books – a huge second-hand book shop in Alnwick's old station buildings. I am in this book shop for the second time this week. Surrounded by all these thoughts – these arrangements of typeface - so much more worthy than my own, I feel overwhelmed. My near-despair is tempered by my joy that so many people actually like real, live books. There is hope for me yet.

I thought I'd get loads of writing done, on this trip. I have jotted and I have been mindful of my surroundings, but I haven't managed to bring my thoughts together into anything shaped or meaningful. Maybe nobody will ever read this, which is a shame. But it's also a relief to indulge in purely therapeutic writing. To unburden my gut, sending myself into spasms, if necessary, I can choose to make it palatable and presentable for public consumption, or I can choose not to. Do I even have a 'public'? Not yet, maybe, but I do have some of the world's passing attention, for a brief flash. Once it's gone, will it be gone? I never know which clichés to cling to and which to mock in an ironic baby voice.

I have never been so at one with winter. I am enjoying draughts and fur hoods around my cheeks. As I battled to drink my bottled water on a wind-buffeted cliff, I watched the droplets being carried away in slow motion, like ash. I have been savouring beauty that my daughter will never get the chance to taste. There is sadness clogged in the treads of my wellies and I don't think I'll ever gouge it out, even with a knife or a pressure-hose. Maybe it's best just to wait until it dries, then bang my boots on the cobbles. I could wear them on my hands and stamp them against the wall like a boxer with anger issues.

I am managing my anger; my pain; the ache. I am managing it like marshy wetlands at the height of the tides. Digging myself channels for drainage, not knowing where the flood will come out if it is diverted. I may need to import pumps from Holland. It says on TV that they have been dealing with wetness for years – that they know how to handle these watery situations. Are all marshes even the same? I should ask – someone must have some kind of answers. My heart feels like a concrete lump, cracking and staining with each new all-time record flood.

In Barter Books, I listen to the jazz which distinguishes this shop from the hush-hush, tap-tap of a library. I am here to buy words. To trade in pre-loved lingo. Dogs are welcome on this ridged, concrete floor, but I have left our Champ in the rented holiday cottage, in contravention of our terms and conditions. The wiry red bars of an electric wall heater blast us all with an unseasonal aridity. There is a vast desert between me and these great minds.

Too many books. I keep my sacrilege silent. It is a well-established fact on Pinterest that there is no such thing. The more shelves, crammed in from skirting-boards to cornices, the giddier the thrill of the heights made possible by tantalising, casually leaning ladders.

In this old hangar, there are stacks and stacks. They climb the walls, sorting themselves into categories as they clock in to the computerised catalogue. Spilling, where they fail to fit – the unrepentant genre-straddlers and too-far-ahead stragglers – into miscellany. Disregarded except by the most dedicated of discount dumpster-divers.

All around me, treatises disintegrate between decomposing leaves, on out-of-reach branches. I try not to heed the screech of attention-seeking fonts – the nagging Dewey chatter. I resist the alphabet's tyrannical demands to be whispered, from start to end, each time a work begs to be put back in its place. Such wicked joy is to be had from inexact, abandoned shoving. My eyes scan over crumpled, scoliotic spines, which stand, slightly less ashamed, amongst untouched, virgin backs disingenuously labelled 'used'. Vintage sells like sex.

Half-term escapees flow over designated departmental lines, tired of fictions fabricated – fresh - for small minds. They gaze upwards, experimenting with an expression that they saw on telly of someone acting interested and intelligent. Hoping that there's more to this world than forsaken foster-kids and famished maggots. Be careful what you wish for. I wish I could go back to my old nightmares of ogres and warlocks.

I cling to the jang-jang-doo of the jazz. The red bars of a wall heater provide me with a background buzz and an extra-arid desert between me and all these great minds, with their crushing knowledge of Smart Food, The Lives of Milton and Pope, Field Sports, Children's Parties, Mother Shipton and Happiness.

These are just the titles I can read with my bad eye, squinting from my position on the stumpy-legged, red velvet-seated, mahogany, carved reading chair, like a dwarf Grimm queen. I am so low. The shelves soar higher, at dizzying, sickening angles. Quotations run around Gothic signage hanging on wires from the rafters - tantalising tasters aimed at those of us who have not yet dared to slip a thumb between the pulpy pages, for fear of committing ourselves to something terrible like finishing something. Dip in.

No-one has written my book, yet. It might be a relief to know that it is out there, closed between dust-jackets, printed in black and yellow, waiting for future niche-purchasers to hunt it down in True Stories and agree that it deserves to be there. No mixing of fact and fiction and no tenuous flourishes, no matter how hard-going the reading is. Dip into me, a bit of a time, like a woman's magazine on a bumpy Intercity, but safe in the knowledge that that you don't need to put on your glasses to check whether the pictures you have believed in have been posed by models.

Royalty, Churchill, Travel, Travel: Britain.

Foreign Languages, all lumped together, are co-existing peaceably enough, for now. I am flying through the streets of this shop. Greek Myths and Bridge Management – singled out for special preservation in airtight chambers - press their noses to the glass, crying out to me to Ask for Assistance. To don borrowed cotton gloves and visit a while, even if it is under supervision, and they know, deep down in their hearts, that they won't be going home any time soon. Priced out of the market.

I swoop down on Casanova and Toadstools. I can see the edge of Fiction. T, U, V, W, X, Y, Z –

contained in a single block, as if the manager lost interest towards the end of the alphabet. On Main Street, Fiction A is expanding into Fiction B. Everyone wants to be in A. Here, the covers defy judgement. Garish images emblazoned with single words - which may or may not relate - give cryptic clues as to what may lie within.

I plump for Contemporary Poetry. Choose two lots. Not exactly blind – one is by a woman I think was recommended on a website which seemed quite reputable. One is by the poet-man I saw last week at a teachers' conference. I blagged my way in. Hoped I wasn't questioned on Literacy Hour or Functional Skills. I like to think that I blended in well, with a quasi-assured face and quizzical arch of the brow that those kids who had 'accidentally' crossed over into Adults would have been proud of. He read from his latest collection, and held up the pages to prove he wasn't making it up on the spot. I wished I'd had my right eye seen to. I could make out black wavy lines, like books drawn in a comic, where the writing would be too small to make out, or the artist thinks words aren't important.

As I queue at the Victoriana till, I flick through, pleased to see that he breaks his lines where I would. I make a last-minute grab for a comedian's memoir of her madness. You cannot entirely trust a memoir. But they had turned her, face-out, and something about the lopsided turn of her mouth over her American teeth speaks to me.

Sunday, 23rd February 2014.

Home again. I didn't want to come home to a home where Georgina isn't. I dropped Paul off at the stadium to watch the Boro match, en route, and the last ten miles were just me and my dog. I struggled to lift my holdall out of the car, so I decided just to unload the absolute necessities. I don't want to give myself the impression that I'm stopping here.

On our last night, we had dinner in the Treehouse restaurant at Alnwick Garden. On this neutral ground, suspended among the branches, we were able to talk. I felt protected by my carefully-drawn eyeliner and multiple coats of mascara. It would have been a shame to have lost my face in public, so I kept it on. Straight.

Paul told me that he wants me to write about Georgina: her bravery, her uniqueness, and our pride. And I do so desperately want to write about her, but I can't quite face it, square-on. There's such a weight to the responsibility of getting it just right. I am daunted by the impossibility of pinning her down onto the page. Should she be captured at all, or allowed to float free in the nebulous rainbow-clouds of our different memories? I could write my own version of my own story, drawing Georgina as an interested observer. I feel what I feel and I notice what I notice; there is no 'correct' interpretation of events.

Paul remarked how much Georgina used to like going to museums, and I thought he must be thinking about another child altogether. 'My' Georgina does not like museums. He summoned up a single example: that, on holiday in Derbyshire, she longed to go to the Knife and Fork Museum. From this he has extrapolated. He has declared this new, absolute truth about our daughter, rubbing out the lines that I myself had sketched. Each person adds a new feature to Georgina's portrait, in a different medium, from a different angle and understanding of the brief. The result is unrecognisable chaos, with brief, odd flashes that nearly approximate a fraction of her.

Such are the perils of group projects. I remember the songwriting session on the Teenage Cancer Unit. I remember how each patient and parent added a new line of their own melody, stretching the lyrics further and further away from the song's theme. In the end, it was nobody's song. In the end, it was barely music at all, though Georgina didn't want me to say so, even afterwards, in private, when I was asked for my honest opinion.

Today, I have only just got up and dressed at 3p.m. It hardly seemed worth it, but I don't want to drag Paul down. I don't want to trigger a chain of phone calls, saying "It's started! The Breakdown's finally on its way!" as if they're announcing a flurry of snow they have been expecting and dreading since November. There is a hanging sense that we cannot get off so lightly. That this moist mildness is lulling us, laughingly, as a blizzard sneaks into the Gulf Stream, unseen, while the weathergirl with the weird fringe and the evening-dress-in-daytime tells us all about the official highs and lows. She is confident that spring is in the air. It can snow in spring, too, as many an iced daffodil trumpet will attest, but she has been asked to put a positive spin on it. We must keep up our spirits. Nobody loves a misery. Above all, we must avoid panic, in spite of the high hysteria and negative thought-count. "Chance of precipitation: ninety per cent", she whispers, when she thinks they have cut to *Homes Under the Hammer.*

How would I write about Georgina? I would use tiny, uncertain letters, printed in soft pencil. How would I sum her up? (Do you want to sum someone up?) Well, she was funny, naughty, principled, pretty, quirky, wise, musical, deep-thinking, and delicate. Did I say funny and pretty? Twice in one week (at A&E and out shopping for holiday clothes), people commented that she should be a model. Then came the sickness. The baldness. The jaundice reaching every cell. And that is what I most remember, right now, except when prompted by photos to focus on the 'Time Before'. Still, the brown eyes were always hers – her dad's, via her grandma. Even when the whites turned yellow.

I wonder, a lot. I wonder if Georgina's enjoying the afterlife. Whether she is at one with nature, since it is in the sky and the sea that I most often see signs of her. I wonder what I will do if I see her again; how I'll know if she sends me a sign. Everywhere, I seek answers, and I draw a blank.

I remember, too. I remember her birth and her living and her dying and her death. Circumstances conspire to remind me that she is gone. The TV is still set to record *America's Next Top Model* and all the (un)reality shows. Nobody has the heart to press the cancel button. I forget. I cook too much food. I buy food which we no longer need in case of impromptu sleepovers. I read a magazine and turn to discuss a new fashion or a controversial issue article with her. I imagine that the noises upstairs are her. For split seconds, I think that I've seen her. Grief does strange things. At the end of the school day, the grief is the worst, as the children file past our house and Georgina does not come tumbling through the front door. From dawn until dusk, grief shifts shape. Yet it is always there, doing its work, even through sleep.

I think about how my daughter changed me, and how I am changed again into something new, now that she has gone. I note that time is still passing and I reluctantly imagine a future. I wonder if I'll ever be happy again, and what on earth that happiness might look like. It feels like a betrayal of her, this keeping on going. This getting by and getting through.

<u>Friday, 7th March 2014.</u>

We have been preparing for my father-in-law's eightieth birthday, with my husband's forty-seventh tagged onto it, the following day. None of us really had the heart. There is no need to visit my mother-in-law in the nursing home, this year, to pretend to be presented with a gift and cake that she cannot possibly have chosen. There is no need for any of it. I noticed a silent tear trace down the birthday boy's face. I uttered "Happy Birthday", ironically and apologetically. It's almost embarrassing that the birthdays haven't taken it upon themselves to cancel.

<u>Saturday, 8th March 2014.</u>

Paul's birthday. He doesn't feel very celebratory. He didn't want a present. Instead, he asked me to sponsor a child in need, for him, so we are now helping a little boy in the Democratic Republic of Congo to stay in school. It's a sticking plaster for huge wounds but it's better than nothing. Paul and I spend the evening at home with wine, crackers and cheese. We almost choke on birthday braveness. Only another hour to go, and we can stop pretending. We can go back to normal – a normal which will never be the same again. Such a glaring abnormality, but nobody detected it, until it was too late. Georgina should not have been that girl.

<u>Sunday, 9th March 2014.</u>

I have been struggling.

I thought it might be post-Northumberland blues or the quick turnaround to get down to London for the poetry prize-giving event by 27th February. I needed to practise to learn my poem off by heart and I had to schmooze. I had to smile when I didn't win. It was a fair decision.

I got terribly worried about leaving my brand new car at the station car park. It was awful to come into King's Cross without Georgina to steady my elbow and steer me through the crowds. It was wonderful and difficult to have her love of London staring me in the face. I wobbled on the escalator, wondering what would happen if I didn't step off at the end. Would I go round and round like on the paternoster lifts in the tower block at university? Would I be able to resist the urge to stick something into the cogs as I went over the top? I felt a rising panic, like the time I lost my mum in the BHS knicker department, back when we still called it Home Stores. I sat outside the Pret A Manger on the station concourse and rocked slightly on the chair, wishing they would put out an announcement for somebody to come and collect me. I wondered who would come, knowing and fearing the answer. I should have gone to Starbucks. You can't go wrong with Starbucks, where the staff call you by name.

I enjoyed snuggling my London niece and nephew, sneaking sniffs of scent that were not quite mine. I wish I had my sister's worries about schools and futures in a dangerous world. It's not envy, exactly. Just wistfulness. At the poetry prize presentation, I told the publisher lady that I'd lost my daughter to cancer and I watched her work out that my daughter must have been too young. I only mentioned it, because she mentioned a poetry collection about cancer, first. I am not a sadist. I may be a masochist.

The stress-rash on my clavicle is bubbling away, in spite of my recent relaxing spa evening. I do not have a bad life, on paper.

As I slept in my London-niece's bed, I recalled all the times Georgina had lain on the airbed on the floor next to me – the time we swapped because her back was hurting her, and my spine was more padded. I thought about the clothes Georgina had bought from Oxford Street, displayed on that bed, ready to be Instagrammed to her friends at home. My niece's room has been redecorated recently, but the space still has that same thickness: rich with city light. The bedroom juts out, above the kitchen, which is the hub of my sister's house. The new wall-to-wall carpets block out the adults' whispers from below, whereas they used to creep through the cracks between the floorboards. The space still felt the same and I was moved to speak to it: to call the emptiness "darling".

I noticed the lime and fuchsia felt owl which Georgina sewed and stuck and stuffed as the chemo chugged into her. A present for her owl-obsessed cousin. I could feel the effort in every irregular tack. I kissed that felt owl.

In London, I also went to a writing workshop at Joe's university. Next year, I will have no business being at that literary festival. Who knows where any of us will be or not be, next year? I met up with Joe afterwards, and he tried not to bristle as I moved in to squeeze the life out of my surviving child. He did an admirable job of pretending not to mind. He took me to his favourite Lebanese restaurant. So sophisticated and cosmopolitan, my son, although I noticed that he still picks out the veg and hides it under his scrumpled serviette. He asked about his dad.

We discussed Joe's twenty-first birthday: he will come home for the weekend but he can't think of anything he wants for a present. I have a child who is no longer young, as well as one who will never grow older. Joe's hair is growing back, now, after his charity head-shave. He had uneven tufts, like owls' ears, so he has given himself a little trim. I wanted to tell him to go to the barbers and get it done properly, but I realised just in time that hair doesn't matter. Nothing does, except him. My son still matters a lot.

We looked around the British Museum, heading for Pre-Roman Italy but we ended up by accident in Clocks and Watches. It wasn't too bad. I made notes about the tilting ball clock and the economic theory which Joe told me is based on it. We stumbled upon Soviet Propaganda Pottery and I told him about the East-Berlin plate I found in the posh charity shop. I am still looking for a place to hang it. We discussed 'Ostalgie' – the yearning for things to be simple, like in the old days. We reminisced about our mother-and-son trip to Berlin for Joe's eighteenth birthday.

Once we'd had enough, we headed to the pub, at Joe's suggestion, but I didn't dare drink alcohol when I still had escalators to negotiate. I remembered to bleep my Oyster Card in and out – still reeling from the deduction of a stiff financial penalty for my hillbilly, rookie mistake in failing to do so on the day I reached London. I walked my son back to his Hall of Residence but he didn't let me in. He hasn't let me see his room there since the first day of the first term when we drove him down south with a packed car and sick stomachs and left him there. He said he's doing fine, apart from this thing with his sister. He's finding his niche. It was time for me to go.

Coming home on the same train as Sunderland fans defeated at Wembley play-offs, I am not proud of the way I pushed and shoved with the best of them at the barrier. I adopted a radical strategy, pushing in at Coach A, which looked full, but was being bypassed by the hoards heading for the far end of the extra carriage. On my own, I was able to slip in, in a way not open to groups. I was able to take advantage of a single, unreserved seat. Backward facing. Window. These are not my usual preferences, but preferences are a silly luxury, in extreme times. The bendy bits by the toilets soon filled up with bags and crouching youths. I had to ask three times for the Sunderland fans to let me get off at Eaglescliffe. They were wearing headphones, drowning their sorrows in hip-hop. *This Service is Alcohol-Free.*

Monday, 10th March 2014.

I slept late. Very late. Almost too late to bother with the day at all. Trying not to let the rest of the day be sucked down by guilt and self-disgust. Today, I will do something. I will start something.

Friday, 14th March 2014.

Four months, now. Facebook goes wild with posts from Georgina's friends, every fourteenth of each month. It's just a number on a screen. My chest aches, as if the sternum has been crushed and is curling inwards, wrapping itself around my most vital organs. I fight to push the blood through.

Joe is coming home for the weekend, tonight. He is coming home to take part in a political campaign, rather than for his birthday, but the reason for the visit doesn't matter, as long as I can hold him. I want to breathe him in. My young. Not so young now. Almost twenty-one years on this planet, outside of me. He no longer smells of our home, but somewhere amongst the London smells clinging to his clothes, I can detect the scent of toddler. Of playgroup and Playdough and Matey bubble bath. I can smell school dinners, even though he usually took a packed lunch.

I am so low. My heart is already buried, somewhere far away. It has been cremated and dispersed on a northern wind. It is washing in and out to shore. I feel that I will go mad if I don't write, but I don't know what I can write that will make anything better. Trust in the process. Trust in anything. Trust in nothing, except the page. I have sent another poem out there, to a publisher, but I can't hear its echo.

<u>Monday, 17th March 2014.</u>

Joe's twenty-first birthday. He stayed over at home for one more night than planned, and we saw him off at Eaglescliffe station. We carried on – the two of us – on the road to Scotland.

Last time we came this way, over to Ayr, we had little kids in the back of the car. They were travel-sick. This time, we took the less scenic, straighter route, even though it meant driving two sides of a triangle. Even though only our coats lay on the rear seat. Even though not even the dog was with us. I felt guilty about our 'freedom'. I don't want this freedom.

We have arrived at Malcolm Sargent House for Children with Cancer, for a Bereavement

Break. This holiday home is run by Clic Sargent, the charity which employs the wonderful social worker who has been helping us. This cannot be my life. I feel a fraud, being offered a holiday here. The staff who greeted us were kind and bright. Our room has a view across the prom and the children's play area. The sky and the sea are silver, and there are shadows of islands in the bay. I look out at spires and at washed-up trees and washed-away walls. There is evidence of a terrible storm, not long ago. Paul and I walked hand-in-hand against the wind. I was wearing the wrong coat. It was too thin and too tailored – impressing no-one.

Rays of sun sneak through, as if Georgina is smiling at us. It reminds me of the smile on her cute, upturned lips when the funeral director carried her body out of the house, wrapped in her new pink blanket. I feel joyful-sad. These rays of sun are the closest thing I've got to evidence that Georgina is following me. Boats chug past the Isle of Arran and I remember the last time we went there, when the children were small. I remember the bleak ferry port. I remember the peace, over the water, even in a heatwave. I can see Arran from our bedroom in Malcolm Sargent House, with my new laser vision.

We are institutionalised, already, by mealtimes and activities and the Fire Exit plans on the backs of the doors. I am aware of the weight of a duvet which isn't mine. I am aware of the gap between our twin beds. There are cream walls, cream sheets and cream valances. There is a hotel-purple carpet.

We have met a couple whose son died two and a half years ago. The mother cannot bear the pain of it, although she still has a daughter. I feel sorry – oh so sorry – for these poor people and their catastrophes. I imagine a giant selecting them and treading on them from on high, like ants. I refuse to admit to myself that we are the same as this couple. We are all here for the same reason: loss. For many reasons: to be nurtured; to be held; to process; to forget; to make sure we never ever forget a single detail.

Another couple has brought their other children with them and I watch them – so little - munching toast and sucking Oreos in the dining room. Do they wonder if their mum and dad will let them be taken, too?

Early bed. I sink into cream-striped cotton that has been washed in Ariel Ultra. I have come so far from home, in less than five hours. I wonder why we are here at all, in all senses of the question. Paul keeps talking too loudly and joking with the staff and guests, whereas I am not in the mood. I know that he's trying to protect us. I love him for his efforts. He is a lost boy. We are lost. At sea.

I miss the turn of Georgina's lip. I miss its curl over her straight, white teeth. I miss her eyes darting downwards and to the side, in the throes of a mischievous thought. I miss her long, silky, slightly-too-bendy limbs and her funny bunion.

When we dropped Joe off this morning, I hugged him. I think he hugged me back. I air-nuzzled his neck and he didn't protest because he didn't want to upset me. I am a selfish woman. Paul didn't hug him at all. He said it wasn't fair, because Joe doesn't like it. In this world, it strikes me, there are 'likes' and 'needs'. I needed that rush of recognition in my nostrils. I needed my fix of child. Joe understood, I think. It will keep me going, for a long time. I didn't stay and watch the train pull in without him and pull out with him in it. It didn't bear thinking about, this departure. Paul and I set off, the two of us, before our son had crossed the footbridge to the platform. We knew he knew where he was going.

Tuesday, 18th March 2014.

Still in Scotland. The rain is beating down against our sea view window. I can't see the island today. I can't see the bay – just grey sea-sky-drizzle, interrupted by a few displays of white gull-aerobatics and stretches of sodden concrete walls, intermittently smashed. The primary colours of the playground are out of place. A single car sits in the coach park, among rusty notices. Aside from two gulls practising their synchronised therm-surfing, wind is the only movement. I know it's there, because a red, plastic baby-swing bucket lurches at the end of a length of rope. My view of the white horses is partially obscured by splatters of wet on the double-glazing. The brass handle is turned down, tight, but I can still hear the roaring. I can still feel the wind-sea's pulse.

Today, I talked to a man whose nine-year-old daughter died, weeks before Georgina. I have never seen such anger, so close to the surface. I could see it coiling round his tongue. His wife just wants to sleep. We all wish we could sleep forever with our sleeping children. I left Paul talking to him - comparing the details of our tragedies. I'd say it was a draw, so far, in the Most Horrible Thing That Could Happen to a Family Competition. They are equally angry with the doctors and with cruel old cancer. They are angry with friends who haven't been there, although they don't know exactly what they'd have liked them to do. I left them sharing tales of their impotence, and of putting on brave faces and not knowing how to stop. I could totally relate, but there's only space for so much agony in one room, even given this building's high ceilings, feature fireplaces, secret panels and nooks.

Just bring our children back. My bed is right by the window. The ships sailing past are like the ships sailing past the window of my childhood, queuing up to be allowed into Teesport. Yet, we are on the other coast. It's hard to know which way round I'm lying. I press my feet against the headboard, and I remember things.

I remember my mum clattering the dishwasher, and sweeping with a hand-held sweeper, so as to be quiet when I – the youngest - had gone to bed. I remember Sunday afternoons, enjoying being alone while Sunday lunch lingered and Sunday tea was still in prospect. Sherry-soaked trifle. Cold Yorkshire puddings. Chicken pulled from glistening wishbones. The shock of the dark meat, shifting me towards vegetarianism. The clouds scurry by, as if they're afraid of being caught and made to stay dangling over me.

Wednesday, 19th March 2014.

What is Gaelic for 'grey'? All the hills, mountains and sea are made of slate. The islands are barely there – watery green-gold. Dying into the grey, grey swell.

Today, we met a seven-year-old who told us about his brother-who-died. It's been fifteen months, now, and their mum recommends yoga to clear the mind. She and I talked about how our loss has made us less fearful, and fear less. We talked about just going for it, and life being too short. She feels that she can do anything, if she can do this – hack this pain – and I know what she means. We admit we're all on anti-depressants.

After supper, I complimented one of the other mums on her new hairdo, and she said she's sick of looking a sight. We talked in the hallway. We moved through to the lounge. This lady I have just met tells me she has suicidal thoughts. When she went outside for a smoke, her husband admitted that he doesn't see the point much, either. None of us are scared of dying. She almost hopes she might find a lump, to speed things up.

She shows me a picture of her late child, on her phone. The little girl looks so cheeky. She reminds me of Georgina, but I don't show my pictures in return. This is not a competition. This lady I have just met says she was okay for the first three months. Then she crashed. Big time. Shaking. Not eating. Not sleeping. Staying in bed all day. When she goes out for another smoke, her husband says he doesn't know how she is managing at all. Paul nods in recognition.

The men have stayed downstairs to chat, and I have come upstairs to write this. There is a strong danger of emotion. Everyone here thinks we are in denial – that we are numb. Long may it continue? I saw myself reflected back in that mother's hollow eyes, but now I can't think of her name. Some might say I have blanked it out. Sometimes, that kind of pain is hard to look at, head on.

Thursday, 20th March 2014.

Lying on my bed, watching the cloud and light show over Prestwick Bay. I watch blue turn to silver, lazing like a dog hogging a sunny patch. The sun has broken through this soaked day, and I know it can't be in Georgina's power to control the weather but I have never been more certain of anything than that my daughter is in those rays – the source of the warmth creeping back into the bones of my feet.

Last night, one of the other bereaved mothers asked me if I ever feel Georgina's physical presence around me, and I said I didn't. Paul thinks he does. I felt envious of their extraordinary senses. But now, in this light that is blazing over the islands, I remember how it felt to hold her. This clarity is almost enough, for now, although it can never be enough. Nothing can. I remember so clearly how I held her hand and her fingers were suddenly so slim and I didn't want her to ever release her grip on me. I remember the change in her fingers, as they passed from life to death. Hard, but still warm. Too still. Not squeezing back.

These few days here in Scotland are bringing it all back. I woke up and it was not all a dream. I never could have imagined a sea so close to absolute black as this one that I see from this window. Nor a sun so white-hot, on the edge of winter. This skyscape - the gulls scraping streaked silver as they dive into mercury – sends my stomach lurching. Is this what they mean when they say they sense them near?

Sunday, 23rd March 2014.

My laptop has crashed, just when I was going to get firm with myself and try to type up my mental and scribbled flittings into some kind of shape. I've been trying to pin down nebulous drifts of ideas. The critical points keep coming to me just before the pills kick in, when my arms are too slowed to reach for the pen and, anyway, Paul wouldn't appreciate the lights going back on. I log my thoughts, trying to think of a memory trick which will help me find the drawer I've filed it in, come morning. I give up, telling myself it will come back to me if it's important. Some do come back, with a bit of coaxing, but I worry about the ones I've let get away – not out of a sense of self-importance, but in case they contain a message from Georgina.

I dreamed that I auditioned for *X Factor* and that they were filming me singing for the part where they laugh at people's self-delusion. Then, Georgina's voice came out of me, and I stared Simon Cowell in the eyes and he wasn't laughing

122

any more. I knew that he'd need me to get my fillings replaced with white ones, but I felt amazed and happy that I could make such sweet sounds. My legs gave way, but they called me back for the next round. They gave me a different coloured sticker and led me out of a different door.

I am thinking about writing a memoir about Georgina's cancer. Except, it would mostly be a memoir about me, because I've now been without her for longer than the four months during which she was ill. It feels wrong for her not to be the entire story, but I can't tell her story for her. I don't know how it felt to be in her position, and I don't know if she would have wanted her story scrutinised. We know that she started keeping a diary, when she was diagnosed. She gave up on Day Three. As far as we know, that is: one day we might discover otherwise. But surely, I have a right to tell the story of a mother's pain, as honestly as I can force myself to write.

When will be the right time to look back on this catastrophe? I will always be in the midst of it – never past or ahead.

Monday, 24th March 2014.

Things are bad. Times are hard. I've come to the new ASDA on the industrial estate, just for a trip out. It's raining, and my shoes are man-made 'suede'. I am not equipped for this weather. I eat Millionaire's Shortbread and watch a group of soldiers blag free cream swirls on their hot chocolate, by charming the canteen girls. It should have cost 50 pence extra, each. The girls put the plastic lids on tight, so that the supervisor won't see the topping. The soldiers laugh, "Help the Heroes". They spoon it into their mouths like kids in an ice-cream parlour. Maybe our troops don't get out much, either. I guess their ranks. I identify the officers by the lack of their free cream swirls.

There is a purpose to this visit: to buy food. As I skate past the pizzas and the crisps and the ice-cream and other unneeded teenager-fuel, I am recognised by a lady whose son knows Georgina. I don't think I know him. She and her friends are running a series of half-marathons, in aid of the Teenage Cancer Trust. She thinks I am an inspiration. I thank her, and I try to make it home without crying. It is damp and grey, even by March's standards.

Thursday, 27th March 2014.

I find myself at the garden centre. Their roof is leaking. Their pots of daffodils are reflected in puddles. My winter coat has been brought back to the front of my wardrobe. Spring was just teasing. The daffodils are in on the joke – their orange trumpets curled into smirks. I want to slash their cheery little necks. Three bunches for £1.20. I can't resist a bargain. I put them in a cream vase on my cream mantelpiece, and those orange mouths follow me around the lounge, opening like baby birds' beaks. Opening wide as they suck up all the water I have provided.

Tomorrow, we are told, will be the start of a two-day heatwave. I am trying to summon up the will to go back to the garden centre, before the rush. It seems insulting to Georgina to be able to think about the garden. It seems insulting that plants can still flower. It is 11.25 a.m. and I put the electric lights on and light two candles, because the daffodils' yellow is not enough.

Saturday, 29th March 2014.

Another month nearly gone and every day takes me further from Georgina. I lie in bed, imagining her arms around me. I stroke the fingerprint which she arranged to be set for me in a silver necklace. How did she keep that secret? I'll wear the grooves away – it's so addictive to feel the pattern of her skin pressing back.

A neighbour's teenage daughter was having a party, tonight. Girls in short skirts spilled out onto the front lawn. There was a thud in my chest as I realised it must be her sixteenth. I felt sick, although I don't want what happened to Georgina to happen to any other child. I have such mixed emotions – including an envy which fills me with shame, and a guilt that I couldn't see her through this world and this life for a full sixteen years.

I have taken a tranquiliser to try to stop the fluttering in my chest and the rats scuttling around in my stomach. It doesn't seem to be working: maybe the doctor gave me a placebo, or they go out-of-date really quickly.

I want Mother's Day to be over and done with. I am still Georgina's Mum. I'm still Joe's Mum. Neither of them is here, but Joe will come back one day, I hope. Joe has asked to come on holiday with us this summer. Does he need to be with us, or is he picking up on our need to have him physically close? I am still a mother-of-two. I dread the day when someone unknowing asks how many children I have. There's no response that's not painful for me. It would be kinder to the enquirer to say "One". But I won't deny my daughter, to save some stranger from embarrassment.

It's getting more difficult, this distance from the memory of the touch of her. I try to hide my pain from Paul, mindful of the danger of bringing each other down to a place we can't climb out of – a deep, dark well with no ladder. Once you're too far below, nobody hears you. And if they could, the rope wouldn't reach you. I try to say the right things to Paul and he pretends to be convinced that there is a need to go on. This is our pact.

My mum told me that she's trying to write a poem about the spring blossom and the garland of flowers Georgina wore in her hair to a festival. Now, I don't want the cherry tree in our front garden to bloom, because I won't be able to bear it when an overnight storm ruins it. And, anyway, I don't know how it has the audacity to flower, now that Georgina's gone. I don't say that to my mother. I tell her it's a lovely idea. Which it is.

<u>Tuesday, 1st April 2014.</u>

(Early hours of the morning) I am watching the 'vintage' music channel. My Mother's Day wine has been consumed. I was going to write "wine from Joe" but it goes without saying that it was from Joe. Georgina can't send flowers or wine, this year. Or ever again.

I watch the vintage music channel, lying on the sofa once more under the multi-coloured blanket that my sister has crocheted for me. These links to the outside world keep me half-whole. The despair has dissipated, for now. It has retreated for long enough for me to drink and listen to vintage Celine Dion and Robbie Williams without real danger of slipping into a dangerous state of mind.

This morning, I spoke to a friend who has mental health problems, and I saw her pain reflected back at me as we swapped stories of our psychiatric prescriptions. We shared a relief that we're both just about getting away with it – not going under. The parameters of normality are shifting: everything's relative.

This afternoon, I spoke to Caytie. I had verbal diarrhoea – I couldn't stop talking because I had her attention and I felt like I might not ever have it again. She seemed thoughtful. She told me about a lad who died young and how his friendship group have marked each event in their lives by including him. I know Georgina's friends will always remember her. We talked about a news report about a teenage girl who was stabbed to death and the memorial party that her friends were throwing for her, twenty years on. When Georgina's friends are in their thirties, Georgina will be frozen in time, like the poor stabbed girl. Georgina will always be fifteen. Only just. Dressed in the fashions of 2013. The music blasts me to the past.

Sunday, 6th April 2014.

Dyeing my hair because my roots are increasingly ashy. How long can I keep getting away with semi-permanent? The snap of the rubber gloves provided with the colouring lotions and potions reminds me of changing Georgina's dressings and cleaning the line leading to her heart. The nurses taught me how to maintain a sterile field, before I was allowed to be in charge of her, at home. To the immune-compromised child, the touch of a mother's skin can be perilous. All procedures must be carried out through regulation gloves, which must be taken from their packet in a strict procedure, so as not to contaminate them.

I eventually got the hang of it: it was something I could do right, even though I'm no more a natural nurse than a natural mother. I learned to mix liquids and shake out air bubbles, and calculate doses. I wished I had paid more attention in science and maths. I managed to stay focused for as long as it took – to keep on not thinking of anything but the task in hand at that very moment.

I part my hair and squeeze the cold, white cream onto the shafts. Drip, drip. The roots drink up the chemicals like a well-known brand of kitchen roll. I home in on the white curlies that sprout almost as soon as I wipe them out. I have aged so much, in half a year. There's no covering it up. I am not a natural brunette. Not any longer. I wait to see the end result and hope for the best. It turns out darker than expected. More chocolate than fudge. It will fade. Nothing lasts.

Sunday, 13th April 2014.

I am aching with need for my daughter. I blast heavy metal from the CD player, trying to deafen myself so that I can only hear Gary Moore's pain. I deaden myself to my own.

It is springtime in the Writing Room. The lawn has had its first cut, but there will be no teenage parties on it this season. The flower pots on the patio need replanting. Last year, I winged it with my gardening. I almost got away with it. The blossom on the apple tree will soon be blown away, but I am going to fill my tubs and my borders with the pinkest, frilliest flowers in the nurseries. I want to look out of the Writing Room's windows and see the flower garland in Georgina's hair.

I can't swallow: I'm surprised that the grief's not dripping from the corners of my mouth. Droplets of despair gather between my cheeks and my gums. It's all I can do, not to dribble.

This week, some of Georgina's friends came to visit. Eleven of them crammed into her bedroom. So brave. So mature. There was a whispered "Oh, God" here and there and the subtle linking of hands or squeezes of the shoulder. It was lovely to see their funny little fashions – their socks rolled down a certain way to display ankle bracelet souvenirs of hot-weather holidays; their skin various shades of manufactured bronze; their eyebrows chalked on (for now, until the celebrities tell them that the make-up rules have been changed).

Nobody really wanted any of Georgina's clothes, as a keepsake. But they took a teddy each, and when all of the teddies had gone, apart from the one embroidered with 'Granddaughter', I felt as though Georgina had moved out to university or London.

Now, Gary Moore's singing "*Empty Rooms*." He says you learn to live without love, but I refuse. Georgina will always have my love and I know that she loved me. I know, because she says so in the song book I found hidden under her bedside table. I also know from the song book that she was scared every time I drove down the street in my black car. She was scared that my depression would take me away and that I'd never come back. She says my car reminds her of a hearse. How frightening for a child to see her mother broken. Her lyrics reverberate with her pain. I read between the lines for blame, but she was just telling her story. Not accusing. Just telling it.

I'm glad that we had the chance to say that the conflict of those years had been left in the past. I hope that that particularly awful darkness stays there. Sometimes, I feel myself splintering. I feel the glue dissolving and the cracks must surely be evident, even to the inexpert eye.

People tell me that this pain is to be expected but that doesn't make it more bearable. People tell me that it's only natural, but it still hurts like hell. People can die from this kind of pain. I feel like I'm giving birth, but in reverse. I need a ventouse. I am struck by an awful jealousy that other people get to keep their kids, even though they may have done a lot worse things than I have done, and haven't even seen the error of their ways.

Joe is home from university. Last night, he asked me to tuck him in, like when he was little. He threw all his bedding on the floor, like a power-crazy baby, and I put his pillows under his head and tucked the blanket around his feet, and placed his old teddy bear, James, under his arm. It reminded me of arranging Georgina, ready for the undertaker to take her body to the funeral parlour before it got light. I remember going to see her, days later, with her tattered teddy Rufus still snuggled next to her. Her slim, pink-nailed hand sank into his plush. There was a bruise. A contusion – "deterioration" – appearing on her razor-sharp cheekbone. The rims of her eyes were red, though they were closed. They took her corneas, for transplants. Georgina wanted this, but I don't like to think about it. There's a lot I don't want to think about. Like the mechanics of dressing her in her funeral outfit.

"Please don't ever incinerate James", Joe says. He is not joking. I won't.

This evening, we are going to my in-laws' church, to dedicate the carved wooden chair that Paul's dad had commissioned in memory of Paul's mother. My poor mother-in-law's death has been obscured, in amongst all of this. What grief Paul must be feeling, losing his mother and his daughter in six months. This evening, we are to go to church and thank God for his mysterious movements.

Wednesday, 16th April 2014.

In a hospital waiting room. Waiting for them to take away my mother's cataracts, I am knocked sick by the sight of the nurse-call button on the wall, with its helpful black-skirted figure outlined on an orange circle. I shudder at the red triangle button next to it, which, if pulled, will get them all here quick-fire – no dawdling of their rubber-soled shoes. I am waiting to take my mother home. She was worried about how I'd pass the time. I'll pass it in the same way I passed seven solid weeks in Georgina's hospital room – with snacks and newspapers and Facebook. Feeling that I'm on public display.

I feel a weight of responsibility for my mother. It is not unwelcome but, if I get her home in one piece, I'll pass her over to my sister who is just up from London with her husband and her kids and a new puppy that lets you carry him round like a baby but is already trying to make puppies with Mum's rescue bitch.

An alarm goes off, down the corridor. I remember the all-night bleepings of Georgina's chemo drip and her feeding tube. How the alarm would go off and someone might eventually come and flick it silent for a minute. How we'd repeat this procedure as another air bubble crept into the system and we waited for 'our' nurse to come back off her break – heavy lidded and heavy-footed - and deal with it properly. Before she'd finished changing the bag, I'd have clambered back into my camp bed and started to drift. In time, you learn to sleep through most things.

I hear the chatter of the nurses. Occasionally, they rein themselves in, as they realise that they are overstepping the mark with the volume or appropriateness of their small talk. It is fascinating how their accents round out, when they come to speak to you officially.

My mother is fine. A cup of tea, and we can all go over the instructions together. All done and dusted.

Friday, 18th April 2014.

Last night, I stayed up way too late, again. I came home from the pub quiz too wired and awake to follow Paul's exhausted steps to bed. I caught up with trashy TV programmes, like the ones I used to watch with Georgina. In spite of the wine I had consumed, I was still sufficiently in possession of my wits to force myself to stay off Facebook. I think I may have overstepped the mark, recently, in terms of commenting with Georgina's friends' posts. I like to keep in touch with them, but I don't want to be creepy. Sometimes, I almost get emotional. I don't want to embarrass them, and I don't want to embarrass Georgina, if she can see me.

Lots of people tell us she is always with us, but I don't know how she can be with everyone who misses her, at once. The cynical part of me says it's impossible but I do see her everywhere. I see her fleetingly, until she turns around and her face morphs into the features of another fifteen year old.

I eventually sneaked under the covers next to Paul. He mumbled, but he didn't ask the time.

I was grateful for that – there have been too many 3 a.m. admonishments and arguments. I lay still, but he sensed that I needed him. He slipped his hand into mine and applied just the right amount of pressure. Love. Maybe it will be okay. I turned towards him and pressed back. I kissed him just enough to imprint on his dreams without startling him. I held on to his hand like a child needing their mother. He cuddled me back, like a child sensing their mother needs them, too. Love. It felt as if Georgina was with us (and it was not embarrassing, even though we were in bed) I am glad that Rufus, at least, was able to stay with her.

I am attempting to give up my wallowing. For days – for weeks - I have been caving in. Slowly losing grip of the promise I made to Georgina that I would keep going. It has been so hard, this keeping going, that I thought it would be easier just to stop. I threw my hands up in surrender to the misery. But allowing myself to stop was a big mistake. There has been panic and there have been nightmares, even though I've been unable to sleep. 'Wallowing' suggests a more comfortable experience: a luxuriant degustation of self-pity. 'Wallowing' suggests a candle-lit bath or lying in the children's pool on a winter break to Tenerife because the shallow water's warmer. It brings to mind fresh sheets or a duvet moulding around your body like baby-powder.

This wallowing has not been pleasant. No, not nice at all. It has been a matter of horror and terror, and of seconds lasting for days and days. It's felt like time has been standing still, and I've only been able to tell that it's actually been passing by measuring the worsening of the pain. A peculiar gnawing, when you don't know whether you feel starving or sick.

I could feel myself slipping back to a place worse than the one I've been trying to forget. I never wanted to go back there but I have been going beyond anywhere I'd ever experienced or imagined. Going to bed at 3 a.m. Getting up at 1 p.m. I have been out of sync with the world – confirmation that this life does not fit me.

I thought I'd take it easy for a few days, but there was nothing easy about trying to sit in one place for longer than two minutes. There was nothing easy about the crawling unsettledness. Agitation. Anxiety. Such inadequate words.

I remember how it was, going through the motions. I remember failing to go through the motions, even though I meant to. Watching myself from the corner of my eye. The awful unease. Floaters. Zig-zag distortions. Too clear. Too bright. Jagged.

After many false starts, I have delivered the promised, much-needed kick to my own butt. It made my teeth clank, but I shuddered out of the place I've been in. I don't know yet which direction I have lurched in, but I sense a shift. I can't stay still. Gotta keep on moving and picking myself up and focusing on my promise. I promised Georgina that I'd be okay, when she wasn't. It was the hardest promise. It seems impossible, yet it is the only possibility open to me. People want me to be 'brave' and 'inspirational'. It's a pressure, but without the pressure I might fall. I have found that taking it easy doesn't work. I need to be hard on myself, to make it through this.

Buying Easter eggs, this year, my basket was emptier than normal. I focus on my twenty-one-year-old son. And my blond, curly-haired nephew and niece.

Sunday, 20th April 2014.

We go through with Easter, for those of us who have been left behind. Joe expresses his disappointment that the Easter Bunny didn't leave Georgina's allocation of chocolate for him. He'd have been honoured to eat her chocolate, on her behalf. There should be some perks to being a bereaved brother. There are no perks, but I hide his eggs behind the curtains and the telly and on top of the piano, anyway, as I have always done. He duly hunts them out. We go through the motions, each of us telling ourselves that we are doing it for the others.

Thursday, 24th April 2014.

Headache.   Everything-ache.   Lung-ache. Can't breathe. I remember lying in bed with Georgina; the final noises she made. Not exactly grunts or groans but a neutral expulsion of air. She was exchanging gases, and then she took none back.

At my therapy group, they talked about being afraid of dying, but I'm not afraid of dying or of being dead, now. I'm afraid of long, drawn-out pain. I'm afraid of everything-ache. Of everything-agony.

I want to write about the things I remember about Georgina, but it's hard to face it head-on. It's as though she's too dazzling to look at directly, like the sun – like the solar eclipse, when we all went out into the office car park to watch it and the manager said "Don't look at it". But those who hadn't got special eclipse glasses just shielded their eyes with one hand, like a Girls' Brigade salute. As if that would protect them, and we didn't dare look for long enough to actually see anything. In the end, we just watched it back on the telly news, afterwards and I always had the feeling that I'd missed something wonderful.

I want to look at photos of Georgina and to play her videos. I want to listen to her CD and all her Mac audio files. I want to be plunged into remembering but I am afraid of the places I might go. I am afraid of going blind and that the blindness wouldn't be temporary. I have shut her bedroom door but I keep peering in. I dash in to snatch clothes from the part of the built-in wardrobe that I hadn't yet handed over to her. She had only just moved in to that bedroom. She had only just put up the canvases of Times Square and the Ramones and chosen the colour-scheme for this new phase of her life.

We had only just risked letting her have the bedroom on the landing which is a little too near to the top of the stairs. We had bought her a special pull-out bed for sleepovers and it collapsed first-time, because eight girls sat on it at once. Their shrieks were captured on video. I am glad, now, for the fashion for selfies – for filming every move and living life on camera. At least we still have the camera. The white voile that we'd only just hung at her new bedroom window still forms a perfect backdrop.

Across the landing stands her little girl's room, with the pink carpet that she chose with her Dad, then smeared with mascara in a failed, pre-pubescent cosmetic experiment. On her old bedroom's turquoise walls, there are butterfly-shaped shadows where she insisted on scattering stickers on the textured wallpaper. At the height of her cabin-bed – which had to be constructed and smashed up in situ – she had scraped off a patch of vinyl bubbles with her fingernails. The butterflies promised to be peel-able and easily repositioned, but we had to use such force to get them off that even the lining paper came away. So Georgina covered the butterfly-holes with song lyrics, which she wrote out and illuminated like scripture. She covered the marks with printed-out selfies and squealed when her brother defaced them with Hitler moustaches. She settled for the caricature that she had done in a town square in Ibiza.

That portrait is dated 2011. The only tinge of colour is the brown chalk dashes of her eyes. The artist exaggerated her lashes and her button nose and the cleft chin that she got from her dad. But the effect isn't comical: the artist couldn't make her look comical. He captured the mischief in the curl of her smile and the sense of promise in the beaded braid she'd had put into her hair at the hippy market. He has sketched her skinny limbs and threaded her wrists with piles of friendship bracelets.

Friday, 25th April 2014.

I've been out to the Happiness Inn for a Chinese meal with my group of friends. One lady has got bowel cancer and she needs an ileostomy. She wasn't there, but the lady who organises the evening out spoke to her. It is reported that she's feeling positive. They don't think that it's spread. I am thinking that it's not such a bad hand of cards. What have I come to, thinking that fifty is not such a young age to get cancer? And that she's at least contracted a 'good' type of the disease?

The Happiness Inn didn't cheer me up much, tonight.

Saturday, 26th April 2014.

Up late. Drinking wine. Watching Vintage TV. The year is 1982: Prince William was born and Sony launched the first consumer CD player. Apparently. Apparently, Elizabeth II opened the Barbican Centre in London. Really? I thought that it was a Sixties construction, because the concrete is so stained. This is what the blurb tells me.

In 1982, I was fourteen years old. I was the same age as Georgina was when she had to cope with cancer. I think of where I was when Adam Ant sang *"Goody Two Shoes"* and Fun Boy Three were all *"It ain't what you do, it's the way that you do it"*. I fancied a boy in my class to death, but it was not reciprocated. I would spin between groups of friends, trying to be popular enough. Trying not to be a swot or - worse – a 'snob' (an occupational hazard of being a teacher's daughter). I try to imagine how I'd have reacted if I'd suddenly been told I wasn't going to live, in a world where fashion and friendships were the be-all and end-all.

Tonight, I saw a video of one of Georgina's friends' fifteenth birthday party. All the girls giggling on the sofas and singing along to a song I don't know. I'm already falling behind with the Top 40. Her mother had captioned the video with a note about absent angel friends. How long before they forget to mention Georgina on special occasions? When they were all posing for photos after the sponsored Fun Run they organised for the Teenage Cancer Trust, last September, Georgina told me it was as if they were already practising for when she wouldn't be there. She hit the nail on the head. I don't want her friends' lives to be blighted, but I want them to remember. I want them to tell their children, so that she becomes a tribal memory. So that everyone thinks they know her, even if they didn't meet her. But not in a Princess Diana-type way.

In 1982, I watched pop videos for clues on how to behave. We didn't have a Beta-Max or a VHS. I watched them live, or I missed them.

I wonder how much Georgina understood. She seemed to grow up overnight. She had an old head on young shoulders – a young head on a suddenly-old body. I think that she understood only too well. More than she should ever have had to. She should have been thinking about eyeliner and skirt-lengths and how to catch that special someone. Had she already met the boy she would have looked back on as *The One That Got Away*?

I hope she felt safe. It's not an age when you want your parents around, except under exceptional circumstances. She told us she realised her mum and dad were her best friends – the ones who truly put her first. It wasn't meant as an insult to her mates. It was just her realisation that her friends were very young. Way too young for this. Her mates were brilliant, but we were older and we managed better, with the benefit of an extra thirty years' preparation for this horror.

I worry about how I'll cope with her friends getting older, when Georgina will be frozen in time, circa 2013 or before. Today, Georgia and Lydia climbed a mountain for her, with a picture of Georgina-this-time-last-year printed on the t-shirts on their backs.

Sunday, 27th April 2014.

Joe has gone back to London. The house is so quiet. Just the two of us, turning the dog back into our surrogate child. I try to make marks in my diary. I need points to aim for – tethers to stop me free-floating away. I cooked Paul his dinner.

Paul has spotted blackbird chicks in the eucalyptus outside the kitchen door. They are camouflaged until the moment they open their beaks as their dad approaches with a worm morsel. They tilt their heads back and they puff up their down. They clamour around him, showing naked mouth membranes. They peck at him like Hannibal Lecter dining on liver and fava beans. Paul set up a chair inside, to watch out for cats while the dad bird fetched more worms. The rain was pattering on the lawn. Ideal worm weather. We can't see the mum. I watched Paul move away, very slowly, because he was scared of scaring the parents away. I love him for caring.

This notebook is running out. It's another sign of too much time passing. Taking me away from my daughter. Soon, I will have a new notebook – one she wouldn't recognise if she saw it in Heaven. I might use the Liberty fabric-covered notebook that the nurses gave her for her birthday. It is untouched. Unopened.

Saturday, 3rd May 2014.

I have been poorly. Diarrhoea struck me during Thursday night. I have been immersed in my illness, even though I can feel it's already passing. I have been lying in bed, thinking about Georgina. Sometimes out loud. I don't know how she suffered what she did. She had no choice but to suffer it, but how didn't she complain more? Did she feel angry at the unfairness? She must have done, surely. I am in awe that she didn't show panic.

Tomorrow, there's a fundraising concert and her friends will be there and I do/don't want to see them. If I'm not well by then, I'll have the perfect get-out / be so angry with myself. I listen for rumblings and grumblings to guess which way things will go with my stomach.

My old school friend's daughter is sixteen today. I remember visiting my friend and her baby-Eskimo new arrival, while Georgina was still growing inside me. Such jealousy is unbecoming.

I understand from social media that Georgina's friend is organising a drinking sesh in the park. I could shake her for ruining her healthy body and yet I sympathise with her need for oblivion. I wish I could join her, out in the cold, on damp-grass, getting rat-arsed. Getting mortalled. Drinking and drinking until a policeman tells me to stop. I have conflicted feelings – it is the first thing but the last thing I want to do.

I have been worried that I'm forgetting little things about Georgina. Some very random things I would like to remember:

- the honking horn noise she liked to make while pulling at her nose
- her calling me "Hezzy Bezzy"
- requiring each individual toe to be "bobbled" when I gave her a foot massage
- my calling her "Binky" after the *Made in Chelsea* lady, because she had long hair and she was classy
- being stuck in a multi-storey car park in Newcastle after the Metro FM concert and Georgina and Amber giggling when I joined the other stranded parents in beeping my car horn in a musical arrangement, to make light of a bad end to a good evening.

Monday, 5th May 2014.

Helen Anderson posted:
So glad I was well enough to enjoy last night's event at the Frigate. What a turnout - we have good friends and live in a great community xxx

Thursday, 15th May 2014.

Last night, I dreamt that Georgina had been murdered. This was so terrifying that I managed to exit lucidly from the nightmare by pointing out inaccuracies in it: that the policeman who came to tell me the bad news could not possibly have my late grandfather's face. I woke myself up and felt around the bed for reality. My hand happened up the silver and crystal angel ornament that my friend Linzi gave me when Georgina died. The cool metal brought me back to earth. Not murdered. Just dead and taken. I shut my eyes and picked up the nightmare where I'd left off.

Friday, 16th May 2014.

It's just over six months since Georgina died, and I need a new journal. I decide to use the one she was given by the hospital staff. It is covered in a blue and orange floral print and ties closed with a coral ribbon. In a way, I feel bad about writing in it, but I don't want to leave it blank, either. I can fill it: it won't be the same words Georgina would have used, but it will be something. Not nothing.

This week, Paul has been in Italy with Big Paul, and I thought that, without him around, I might be able to 'let go' as I wouldn't need to keep on going for his sake. I planned a mini-collapse but I couldn't quite summon it. There were a few times when I was on the brink of tears; a little talking-out-loud to Georgina around the house. But no big purging of grief.

144

On the fourteenth of the month, I went to the beach, to try to be 'with' her, but I just didn't feel her there. I wish that she had wanted a grave. It wouldn't have been a chore or a duty for me to visit it – it would have been a pleasure. Well, not exactly a pleasure, but an act of remembrance and connection. A grave might have become a public shrine, and I didn't want that, either – teddies soaking in the rain alongside faded plastic windmills.

Although Georgina's ashes are scattered by the boats, I can't make myself stay on the beach for long enough to feel that it means something. I splodge along the water's edge with the dog. I look at the grains of sand and I wonder where the parts of her have been carried, by now. When she was alive, I used to like to keep track of where she was. So now it's hard to give her this freedom to go wherever the tide might take her. I'd like to sit in the sand dunes and stare up at the sky, but it's not private enough. I'm aware of the other walkers watching me. I know that I couldn't cry for long without someone coming over and expressing concern. Or scurrying by and surreptitiously calling the police or whoever it is that one reports distressed, bereaved mothers to.

I long for wide, open spaces. Alien environments. Nothing but me and the ground and the sky. Then, perhaps, I could let go. Then, perhaps, I could let my girl go. I could begin to loosen the apron strings, but I feel naked without them bound around me, tight.

Sunday, 18th May 2014.

Shopping in Middlesbrough. Georgina's voice emerges from the mall's tannoy system. It is confident and definite – a clear record that she lived. I am so grateful that the management are still playing *Two Thirds of a Piece*. Her friends often message me to say that they heard it and that it stirred them and soothed them. I stroll up and down the central arcade, window-shopping, until the final, final chord is struck. My daughter's voice stretches out one note into infinite length. I drink in the sub-notes: entire songs within a single beat.

Wednesday, 21st May 2014.

Chloe's year group are leaving school. I've seen them hanging around Sainsbury's in their leavers' sweatshirts. Chloe's hair is growing back. She reports on Facebook that she can get it into a ponytail.

Last night, Paul and I went to the Freemasons' Hall, to be presented with a charity cheque. I spent hours – more like days – obsessing about what to wear, until Paul found a picture of the previous year's dinner on the internet, and I was then reassured that black trousers and a floaty pink blouse would be a fitting ensemble. At the event, I enjoyed people talking about Georgina but I was less happy with the perpetuation of the myth that her last few weeks on earth were an "exciting" time for her. Paul seems to think that this is true, even though we have spoken – had words – about it.

We were showing the Masons designs for a possible new Teenage Cancer Unit, and the sight of those drop-down parents' beds filled me with misery. I would give anything to lie at the foot of Georgina's bed, if she were still in it. Paul is still angry with her oncologist but I don't think that anyone could have stopped that cancer. I'm angry with the cancer, but it was part of my daughter and I am not angry with her. This is where adversarial language about 'battling' cancer falls down. Georgina battled and battled, but was hopelessly outnumbered. It was the cavalry against tanks.

I am angry with everyone – irritable with Paul for leaving me. For going to Italy with Big Paul and making me cope alone. Then coming back. I was so relieved to see him come home, but I've done nothing but grumble at him ever since. His jokes are not funny and he doesn't draw the curtains back symmetrically. All this is true, but doesn't warrant the venom that I'm throwing at him. I am angry with some of my friends and relatives for not enquiring how I am and for the lack of thoughtful texts or cards or surprises to raise my spirits. Do they think that my pain has dissipated already? Do they think?

I'm grateful to old friends for showing me that they're keeping me in their thoughts, even when their own lives are busy and complicated. I'm grateful for the new friends who have come forward to offer support and who have really meant it. I feel like shunning those who have abandoned or aggrieved me, but I know that that will only make things sadder. It is tempting, though: I am convinced that the shunning would give me great satisfaction, in the short-term.

Nothing matters and everything matters so much more than ever. I switch between not caring and caring so deeply that I am filled with a huge rage. I dream about being angry and telling people what I think. It's a nightmare, this dream. It's a distinct possibility. I put these thoughts on hold, because I don't trust my own judgement right now. I keep making mistakes. Forgetting things. Changing my mind, then changing it back again. Not having a mind at all. I was only just finding my mind, and now I'm losing it. I cling on to my sanity, tight, as I promised Georgina I would.

Sunday, 8th June 2014.

Helen Anderson posted:
Wonderful weekend in Shropshire with 'old' friends Meg and Rob and their beautiful daughters and crazy hound xxxx

Monday, 9th June 2014.

This morning, I set up my notebook and pen at a table towards the back of a coffee shop in our village. A group of ladies who were sitting on the sofas next to the front window were talking about difficulties they were experiencing with their children's autism. I had every sympathy with them: the autism gene runs determinedly through our family, and I know first-hand about some of the challenges it presents. I tried to get on with my own writing project, but their voices carried so that I couldn't help but pay attention to their conversation. I must remember that that café has excellent acoustics, next time I'm organising a spoken word event.

Next, they started loudly agreeing that it would be easier if their kids had cancer, as they would get more help from the health and social care services. All the money that should be spent on learning disabilities and child mental health is spent on kids with cancer, they claimed, whilst even Asperger's can be just as deadly because it makes you depressed and suicidal. There has been a lot of negative publicity on Facebook about a book called 'I Wish My Kid Had Cancer' (as opposed to autism) and I couldn't believe that they were still perpetuating the story that kids with cancer get 'all the attention'.

I tried to distract myself by making notes about my surroundings, but I could hear the blood rushing in my ears. I was shaking so much that I had to abandon my untouched coffee and scone. This was serious. I kept making my mind up to say something but nothing came out. I made up my mind to leave. I didn't totally trust myself to pass them without exploding, but I politely approached them and said that I couldn't help but overhear (I really couldn't!). I told them that - since I have experience with both - I could personally assure them that parenting and losing a child with cancer is definitely harder than coping with autism.

I did say I have sympathy with their difficulties, but that I found their remarks ill-informed.

One of them mumbled about it being a private conversation and the others looked at me as if I were an alien. Only one said that she was sorry. I wobbled my way home, trying to maintain my composure. I burst into tears at the sight of my own front door and I had to stop Paul from going straight up to the café to tackle them. I have been worrying that my reaction was over-the-top, but most people I have told about it have said that I dealt with the situation with astonishing calm.

I can't believe that there are people out there who think that a child with cancer is 'lucky'.

I don't know whether I'll ever be able to show my face in there again. I probably spoilt those ladies' morning. They certainly put a dampener on mine. Maybe it all went completely over their heads, or they think I'm a ridiculous hysteric, if they remember me at all. I like to think I made them think. Next time, if they really must spout off, maybe they might lower their volume. They are lucky that they didn't slip up in front of a 'cancer mum' who has not been brought up to be as polite and non-confrontational as I have. There are a lot of angry cancer mums out there. Those autism mums might be aggrieved and fierce, but they should watch out.

Sunday, 18th June 2014.

On the train to London. Tonight, we meet up with Joe at Gatwick, and tomorrow we fly to Toronto, for a week's holiday. I am always on the move. Paul and I booked seats opposite each other, but we moved to backward-facing, adjacent seats, so that we can spread out a bit. I am aware of moving backwards. It makes me feel sick, to write. My hair is tied off my neck with a rubber band. It tugs at my temples. I notice the weight of Georgina's silver fingerprint, resting, skew-whiff, on my breast.

Ssh: Quiet Coach. Please be considerate to other passengers.

Thursday, 22nd June 2014.

The CN Tower needles a blue, humid sky. We are at a festival on the shore of Lake Ontario. Paul is napping in a much sought-after patch of shade, his head resting on a drugstore carrier bag. He twitches like a dreaming Labrador. Joe leans back against me, engrossed in his phone. His scalp is turning pink. His thumbs dart around the black slick of the screen. I watch honey-skinned girls in floaty dresses and nut-brown-limbed boys in baggy shorts pass by. I ponder the takeaway food opportunities: corn, coconut, curry, pies, and Oreo pastries (made to order). Those cool-box toting parents who had the foresight to bring a picnic from home steer their children firmly past the stalls. There is a queue to get your caricature done. I am so glad that we have our caricature of Georgina, sketched by a street artist in an Ibizan market-place, three long years ago.

Friday, 23rd June 2014.

On a train from Toronto to Niagara Falls. We trundle through the suburbs. Taco Bell, Kendo Sushi. Silver City, Chorizo. This train actually says "Choo", like a runaway train in a song. Esso. It's early morning but you can tell that it's going to be another scorcher. Canyon Creek Chophouse. Overhead wires string the sky together. I think of Georgina, setting out strands of threads on her hospital bed tray, and fumbling to plait them into friendship bracelets with nerve-damaged fingertips. I remember her stocking up on her craft supplies from the activities lady, reasoning that the friends who came to visit her at the weekends might feel more at ease if they were occupied. Union Pacific. Go Transit.

I peer past Joe's new straw hat to watch the apartment blocks shrink to two-storey, clapboard houses with porches and verandas. The train choos at every level crossing – at every track that cuts across the red-earth of the vineyards. I remember Georgina's honking-thing – all the times she asked if we were nearly there, yet.

Wednesday, 28th June 2014.

Helen Anderson posted:
Please download A Song for Georgina – written by Simon Galloway and performed by Jamie Graham - available from tomorrow. I've heard it and it's beautiful - kind of sad, but also uplifting xxxxx

Friday, 4th July 2014.

Last night, I semi-slept for about four hours. I felt fuzzy butterflies crawling on my skin. When I opened my eyes, I saw red and black butterflies and a miniature elves' workshop, where the cream bedroom wall should have been. I knew that I was hallucinating.

I dreamt about Georgina: the detail of her hair being tossed and her lips breaking into a smile. I felt her arms around me. Her limbs were soft and slim, and I knew that she was real. She told me so, and at last I knew how it felt to believe. In my dream, I thanked her for showing herself to me. She spoke, and I remembered how much I'd forgotten her voice, with its sweetness and its little cracks.

I tried to wake Paul, to alert him to Georgina's presence. I forced out a sound from my throat and I think it may have broken through my semi-sleep. I knew I was far away, but I felt him move, next to me, under our too-hot, medium-weight duvet. In the morning, he said that I didn't wake him, and I say nothing: it is too difficult to explain what he missed. And he might smile, but he would worry about my mental health.

I knew that my daughter was there. She appeared to me. But so did the butterflies and the elves. So now, I have to believe in butterflies and elves.

<u>Monday, 7th July 2014.</u>

Saturday was the Memory Day organised by the children's cancer ward. It was sunny. We sat on the grass while they played Ellie Goulding and Lily Allen and read out the names of all the children who have died of cancer in this tiny corner of the world, over the course of the last ten years. Having an 'A' surname still has its advantages when you're dead: Georgina Louise Anderson was one of the first names to be read out. We placed a single pale pink rose in the middle of the heart-shape marked out with ribbons on the lush lawns. I was glad that it was suitable weather for sunglasses. We pinned Georgina's photo to the noticeboard in the marquee. We recognised the name of a tot who had trundled up and down the ward with a huge lump on his head. He made Christmas and his first birthday. I recognised his dad. In hospital, we never talked, but we did now, now that we have this further unwanted connection. Paul didn't want to talk to Georgina's consultant, but I didn't want to ignore him. We had not always seen eye-to-eye with this doctor but he is a good man. He looked sorry that we didn't approach him, but he kept a respectful distance. Keri, the Macmillan nurse, helped me chase after the consultant. He held his arms out to me and I cuddled in. It felt better than holding a grudge. Paul shook his hand and they joked, "No hugs". Nobody mentioned the virtual (e-mailed, complaining) elephants in the room. We were not in that filtered-air hospital room – we were outside on a sunny July Saturday.

Paul and I tied the strings of our white balloons together, and they floated high, still joined, with their message-tags waggling. It reminded me of our promise to stay together. I had been a bit (okay, very) mean to Paul, on the way there. I think it was all the memories of bedside bickering getting stirred up, in anticipation of seeing faces from that terrible era. I accused him of being uncaring and I brought up ancient grudges. I said sorry, as I watched my balloon cling on to Paul's. He said to forget it and I felt back on track – reconnected with my promises to my dying daughter.

Today, I went to the cemetery because it's my dad's birthday. On the way there, the sun turned into rain – light splodges of warm, summer rain. I could hear Dad saying "Just a passing shower", like he did when he was judging whether to make a dash to unpeg the washing from the line or to hope that the sun would soon be back to dry it again. I parked up at the gates and I got out. I set about sorting the flowers Mum had left on his grave, deciding which ones had drooped beyond the point of salvage. I shuffled the stems around, trying to keep the arrangement symmetrical, as Mum left it before she went off to visit her brother. It was colourful – the only way my dad liked flowers to be. No wishy-washy, creamy whites. I added yellow chrysanthemums to Mum's hot pink gerberas and red roses. I gave the vases a quick wipe over with some moistened paper towels, so that the "In Loving Memory" was legible and unmuddied.

I left my dad's grave looking smart. I, however, was bedraggled. The shower did not pass and it had poured on me until my blouse went see-through. I turned the car air con button to 'heating' and blow-dried my body. Just up the road, it was still dry. I imagined Dad trying not to laugh. I imagined him breaking out into a snigger and how I would try to stay annoyed. Back home, Joe wouldn't believe there'd been such a downpour only two miles away. He says he can remember his grandad always saying "Just a passing shower", so that he didn't have to get out of his armchair to deal with the laundry on the line.

I meet up with a local lady, who I'd got to know on Facebook. She's a young widow and she blogs about it. We share grief of different kinds. There is a name for people like her, but none for those in my boat. I feel almost widowed and orphaned, though, thankfully, I am not yet either. But a term is definitely needed for one who has lost her young. There ought to be a single word to encapsulate this position into which I have been forced.

Tuesday, 15th July 2014.

About to set off to Darlington to catch the train to London, for Joe's graduation. His results haven't been issued yet. We are almost sick with nerves and with trying not to show it. It doesn't really matter how he does, but it seems important to him. It would be nice for all his efforts to be recognised.

I remember how we filled the time while we were waiting for Georgina's scan results. Sleeping or busied with the business of her tubes and her medicines and her massages and her feeds and her trips to the toilet. Not forgetting those rubbishy telly programmes. Last night, I sat with Joe and watched *Jail* and *Traffic Supercops* (or something like that). It was junk food for the brains, keeping our minds just full enough until bedtime.

I'm nervous about Joe's results, but it's amazing how losing a child gives you a sense of proportion: Joe's exam results will affect his life but at least they won't take it.

Thursday, 17th July 2014.

Helen Anderson posted:
Just back from a whirlwind couple of days in London. Joe got his final results just as we were arriving at King's Cross, the day before his graduation! A First Class Hons degree, with a special departmental prize for his dissertation. We already knew he is a clever lad, but he has worked really hard to get this, particularly under the difficult circumstances of this last year. Catching our breath before we think about finding him a flat for starting his new job in September!

Thursday, 17th July 2014.

On the train home from Joe's graduation in London. He got a First. A special prize for his dissertation. Afterwards, we went into a wine bar in Covent Garden, to dine with our new graduate. It was a little place Joe knew and really recommended. It turned out to be a little place his dad and I used to frequent when we were first married – only a couple of years older than Joe is now. Things had come full-circle. Finally, a nice, positive circle.

It is a year since Georgina's cancer was diagnosed. At the post-graduation cocktails, another parent asked us if we have any more children and Paul said "No, we just have Joe." We didn't want to make everyone feel awkward, on a happy occasion. Watching the students all dressed up for this special day, I felt sad that it would never come for Georgina. I feel sad that we won't get to see the beautiful young woman she was becoming.

I worry that Georgina was terribly scared and felt she had to put on a brave act for our sake. She was definitely scared when they confirmed her tumour was malignant and said she had to stay in hospital for a biopsy. But she asked sensible, probing questions, while Paul and I quivered. Two days later, she was reassuring her friends at her belated 'end-of-term' party.

I am trying to be happy for Joe. I am happy, but happiness, from now on, cannot be what it was in the past. I am proud of my son. But I am frightened for him and worried about what might snatch him away, like when he was in the womb and I willed him to cling on, knowing that one blow or one mutant cell could be the end of everything. This is a HAPPY day.

Tomorrow, we are going into Georgina's school to discuss an annual prize to be awarded in her memory. We have been trying to think of a fitting tribute, but none of our ideas quite cut it. We hope that the new head teacher will help us formulate our thoughts – that he might have suggestions, even though he did not know our daughter. Time is taking us away from her. I am scared that her room is losing its smell of her. If she had lived, she would have changed, by now. They do, don't they, at that age? Not my daughter – she won't ever change, for anyone. I follow her friends on social media, but she might well have had new friends.

Each time I return home after a trip, it hits me a bit harder that she is not waiting in that house. And that house feels a bit less like home. People like to talk about the money that has been raised for charity, in her name – about the 'good' that has come out of this tragedy – but nothing can ever be good enough to compensate for such absolute devastation.

I need to ban myself from playing the "This-Time-Last-Year" game. This time last year, I consoled myself that, this time next (i.e. this) year, it would all be over. But like this? How did I not know that it would end like this?

I read that a baby who was on the ward at the same time as Georgina has died. His mother was a force to be reckoned with – filling the parents' kitchen with her loud news of her little boy's progress. There is to be no more progress for him, and I am gutted. His first birthday – the birthday cake they dished out in hospital – was his last. That baby used to point at food and shout and peep over his dad's shoulder. I don't know much else about him. Did he have enough time to build up a biography? Can such a short life be a full one? I wonder how his parents will cope, stretching eighteen months of memories to last them forever.

Friday, 18th July 2014.

Just had an emotional moment in WHSmith, looking for a Congratulations card for Joe and 'Two Thirds of a Piece' drifted in from the Cleveland Centre. — feeling weird.

Monday, 4th August 2014.

Helen Anderson posted:
Exciting times for Amanda Bell, due to set off on her cross-channel swim in four hours! An amazing lady - I hope all her hard work and preparation pay off xxx

Tuesday, 5th August 2014.

Helen Anderson posted:
Amanda - you are one very special lady. What a tribute to my special little lady. Thank you so much and congratulations! Xxx

Saturday, 9th August 2014.

For his twenty-first birthday present, we offered to pay for Joe to go on holiday. He has chosen Germany. He loves Germany. I am invited and I accept, in spite of Joe's dismissal of my suggestions that we go to Barcelona, instead. So, we flew to Düsseldorf. Not an obvious choice – most definitely Joe's.

We have taken the train to Köln and sit by the Rhine, looking over to Deutz. The Race for Life is going on here, too. Purple-pink t-shirts bob along the riverbank to the soundtrack of drummers and supporters' whoops. The runners wear pink grass skirts and pink tutus and pink wigs. I somehow don't find wigs entertaining any more, after my battles with Georgina's. The race flows in the same direction as the Rhine. At least I think it does, but when I stare at the water for long enough, it appears to ripple in the opposite direction. Barges piled with gravel and pleasure boats piled with partiers sail by. And still more purple-pink t-shirts, making remembering dead relatives seem like such fun. Some are walking at the back. Some obviously set out to walk, brandishing Nordic poles.

A bride and groom eat pizza and drink ale in a café in the main square. A baby is being taught to chase pigeons, so that its parents can take staged photos of the chaos. A stag party pops open a bottle of champagne. They have brought plastic cups and a cool-bag. They try to hide the bottle when the street-wardens patrol by. A group of hens stagger by.

"Sssh." They point to their stash of bottles amongst their picnic. "Sssh. Come drink with us."

Joe presses me to taste traditional Kölsch beer. I am not a beer drinker. He says I won't regret it, but his eyes flash with glee at his anticipation of my grimace. I prefer it to the dark, spicy Altbier he made me try yesterday. Sure enough, he looks disappointed.

The flow of purple-pink has stopped. Everyone has forgotten about cancer and gone back to drinking and smoking and sunning themselves silly.

<u>Sunday, 10th August 2014.</u>

Daytrip to Wuppertal. We visit Josef Engels' house – or where it was before the bombs flattened it. Sadly, the Museum of Early Industrialisation is closed for improvements, but we are still able to view the Communist Manifesto in multiple, Soviet-sponsored languages. Joe tells me that he likes 'true' communism, but not what it later became. He wants a photo with the Engels birthplace plaque, but not with the stylised Soviet bust which was commissioned to stand alongside Marx and Lenin. How we all tiptoe around our past, and try to find acceptable language for it – a history we can live with. How we pussyfoot around pain, leaving its edges raw and unhemmed so that it forms a fragile, keloid scar – connective tissue devoid of elasticity.

I am drinking cappuccino in a station café of a German ghost-town on a drizzly Sunday afternoon, all because of something somebody thought and bothered to express on the page. The seats underneath the outside canopy are taken. Taxis queue to take the odd new arrival away. The national flag is being flown from a third-floor balcony, as though the window box in which it is staked were an allotment or an ambassador's garden. A taxi-driver's girlfriend sits in the front passenger seat, chatting to him while he waits for jobs to be called in. This is my son's idea of a vacation.

Tuesday, 12th August 2014.

Home again. So lonely, living in a house full of men. So irritable, claiming that I never have time and space to myself. I can see why married couples migrate to separate bedrooms, and it has nothing to do with sex. Paul and I have been a couple for twenty-nine years, and we could both do with occasional respite. It's a balance: if you separate for too long, then you don't even have shared experience to clag you together. I'd like to talk about something we haven't discussed before – to hear a new story. Grief is making me restless.

Tuesday, 12th August 2014.

Helen Anderson posted:
Paul and I met another group of great young people at the NCS at Redcar, today. We talked about cancer and Teenage Cancer Trust and Georgina's story and they are hopefully now inspired to get going with their Social Action projects. Can't wait to find out what they come up with...

Thursday, 28th August 2014.

Joe has left home. Properly. His dad has gone with him on the train and they're getting a taxi from Argos to his new flat, with his new necessities. He has graduated to a double bed, after three years in a single room in halls of residence. He needs a new duvet and four Fogarty pillows. He'll be able to stretch out. He will find his bed at home cramped, even if the memory foam is still moulded to his shape.

I want to let him go and I want to keep him forever. This is my punishment for thinking "They don't grow up fast enough" when people used to look at my offspring and warn me "They don't stay little for long." Those tea-times, when the children were small, I would be waiting for Paul to come home from work and he would seem to take forever. Everything seemed slow and difficult back then. Every Wednesday, it was my neighbour's day off and I would notice his car on the driveway and marvel that I'd made it through another week. Every week, for quite a while, I'd feel certain that when the next Wednesday came round, it would do so without me. I'd be surprised when I eventually witnessed time clicking over into Wednesday morning again. Those weeks seemed so long. I wished them away.

I walk the dog and he is old and ambling. Soon, we will have to lose him, too. I set off upbeat, although his 'morning' walk doesn't start until 12 30 p.m., by the time we have both rallied. I bump into a lady who used to be toddler Joe's favourite server in the local ice-cream parlour. She stops to ask after him and to tell me again how much she used to love his infectious grin and his little-old-man questions. I report that this is a momentous day and that Joe is doing well. I know where this conversation is going, but I don't head it off quickly enough. I should have kept on walking.

"How old's your daughter, now?"

There it is. I try to break it gently.

"I wasn't sure if you'd have heard, but unfortunately she died recently."

Her falling face. My need to be bright and brave and assure her that it's alright. That we are surviving. She looks at me as if I'm inhuman.

"But there must be times when it gets to you".

I obviously act too well. My outside doesn't let my insides show through. If Georgina had (God forbid) been murdered, my impassive, overly cheery face would be indisputable proof of my guilt.

This lady has heard about Georgina, because she now works in a neighbouring school and the kids were talking about it. But she had not connected her name to our family. We are faces to her, rather than full names. In her mind, Georgina is a tiny tot in a shiny pink anorak, whilst Joe is a chubby schoolboy with chewed cuffs, coming up to the counter to order with my dad. She is nearly crying. I answer her questions about symptoms and dates and treatments. I answer so brightly that I almost fool myself.

Next week, a school year will start without Georgina being part of it even for the couple of hours she managed last year. Her friends are getting taller. They are buying new clothes.

I am angry, again. I'm not talking about Georgina's friends, here, but I can't stand it that some people who don't look after their kids but let them stay out all night and post filthy language on the internet get to keep their daughters, while mine – who was cherished and fretted over and collected by her dad at midnight – gets taken.

I listen back to the radio interview that we gave when Georgina was in hospital and her song was released. I listen to myself calmly stating that there are no other treatment avenues open to her and that we are focusing on taking her home. How hard it must have been for her to hear that. My calm tone – designed to instil calmness in Georgina – gives me cold shivers. Shudders. Georgina is already talking about herself in the past tense.

"It's good to have stories to tell the nurses about the kinds of stuff I used to do."

She is already looking back on her life, when she has only just turned fifteen. They say they grow up too fast, nowadays. She grew up in those four months when she had cancer. It was as if she had been struck with a super-aging disease. Suddenly, she had the body of an old woman, but only a child's years officially clocked.

I am sitting in the sun in jeans and a vest top. I bask, between blasts of North wind. The French doors to my writing room are fastened back but they slam shut, anyway. I am like a Brit on a winter sun-soaked Canarian balcony, where all the locals have succumbed to woolly jumpers but I am still squeezing out every last solar drop. I don't want to look ahead to the winter because another winter without Georgina seems unfathomable. But it will come round again, soon enough, like those Wednesdays of old, and I will probably have survived.

Sunday, 31st August 2014.

Helen Anderson posted:
Good luck to Joe, starting his new job in London tomorrow. Very proud of my boy xxx

Tuesday, 2nd September 2014.

Back to school for some, but not for Georgina. She won't even get to take part in two days of this academic year. I remember her chubby legs poking out from grey pinafores, and lacy knee socks and Clarks shoes. I remember morning discussions about hair bobbles and styles. I worry that I am just remembering photos, but I can definitely remember, first-hand, parting her hair, which insisted on arranging itself into a zigzag, rather than a straight line. I remember wondering how much of a kink was tolerable, and when I needed to brush the whole thing out and slice through the brown strands again with a comb, from scratch.

I have been to the doctor's about earache, again.

"How long have you been deaf?" she wants to know.

"About a year."

"And you only thought to mention it now?"

No, I mentioned it to a different doctor in July and to another locum, last week. I cannot tell this story again.

"Are you stressed at all?" Her smile is kind, bordering on patronising.

"Yes, very. My daughter has died."

She looks up from the computer screen.

"How old?"

"Fifteen." I have to practise saying this, because she's barely fourteen, in my mind. I anticipate her next question. "Cancer."

"I heard we had one of those but I didn't know it was your daughter. Condolences." One *of those.* Sometimes, I wish I had selective deafness, to filter out crass remarks.

My ear appears to be infected, and I have to come back in a week for a review. It's probably nothing, but it is a puzzle.

She wasn't to know that I have heard those words before, there, in exactly the same room. This doctor is a round, black lady, but at that moment I see a skinny white, man-doctor, telling my daughter she's too young for gallstones. Probably nothing.

I tell people that I don't blame that doctor who dismissed Georgina's pains. I suppose he's sorry. I suppose a lot of doctors would have done the same. I tell people that I am fine, apart from the earache and the deafness, which I'm finally admitting to, now.

<u>Wednesday, 17th September 2014.</u>

I dream I am on a clifftop path in the South of France, trying to take photos of the bay, but every time that I get my camera on my phone to focus, someone walks in front of me. I get into an argument with one of the culprits – a man with dark, flashing eyes. I feel the anger in me rising, and I am afraid of myself. My big brother (who – bizarrely – happens to be with me) apologises for me. "Sorry, mate. Thanks, mate." I am furious with him for diffusing the situation. I want to let rip.

In my dream, Paul and Joe are playing football on the beach below, and I hear a smattering of French words over a tannoy.

"That means 'tidal wave'." I didn't even know I knew that word, in French: it's a very specialised vocabulary of disaster. I know I know "flood" and "storm." All the tanned people are leaving the beach, but Joe and Paul keep on playing. My view is clear, now. I frame them, with pink geranium flowers as foreground. There are pastel houses and a church spire to my left. To the right, on the flat, golden sand, lie two pairs of flip-flops and my black, winter handbag. I don't think they've been keeping a proper eye on my bag. If I've lost my diary, I'll never know who I am.

The sea is azure (as in "Cote d'Azur" – the holiday Georgina never got to go on). It sucks itself out towards the horizon. Before the fake shutter on my camera phone fake-clicks into place, the passers-by start getting in the way again. There's a constant procession, with beach mats and pop-up tents on their backs, as if they're fleeing genocide. I can't even see the beach, for their heads. I hold the phone up high, like a kid filming a concert, but I am jostled. I have poor balance, and it is a vulnerable stance. As I fall, I put my hand out to save myself. I wake up on the bedroom floor. I wake Paul up with my gasping.

Tuesday, 23rd September 2014.

So many thoughts and feelings at the funeral of one of Paul's former colleagues today. His daughter, who is fifteen, read out a poem that she'd written about her dad. It had some slightly clunky rhymes in it, but it was perfect. Her voice broke twice, but she didn't cry. She was amazing. It was quite a long poem. The last funeral I went to before this one was my daughter's. It was only Georgina's second funeral ever. The second in six months, after my mother-in-law's. I'd like – I need – to write a poem that's directly about Georgina. It's something I must have been avoiding. Her funny idiosyncrasies lend themselves to poetry.

After his colleague's funeral, Paul and I spooned on the sofa and I listened to the click of his mechanically-assisted heart. The last person I held like that was Georgina, in her hospital-at-home bed. I listened to her breathing, and I was thankful for it. It stopped.

This was my first Roman Catholic funeral. I enjoyed 'Ave Maria' and I knew the words of the first hymn. There was incense. Body and blood. Paul and I want humanist funerals: we discussed it, on the way home, before the spooning.

Now, he and Big Paul are watching a football match on Sky in the lounge, and I am alone in my Writing Room (I am still trying to call it that again) facing the wall where my daughter died. I am humming along to Alison Moyet. I hear near-misses in the lounge. I have logged off from Facebook. I have logged off from editing my novel. I have logged off from my scented candles and from the stars through the skylight. There is a last-minute goal-roar. I wish I believed. It might be comforting to take Communion and to genuflect when things get scary.

Friday, 26th September 2014.

I spent the morning in bed. Last night, I couldn't sleep, and at 3 a.m. I pulled on my nightshirt and told Paul that I was going into Joe's room – that I was taking another sleeping pill. Not to worry if I didn't emerge for a while. I lay down on Joe's memory foam mattress, which groaned as if it were still missing him. I shuffled into the hollows he has left, as best as I could, and I waited for sleep. The single layer of the blanket over me reminded me of sleeping by Georgina's bed when she was ill. I wanted them both. In this last year, there have been so many strange and makeshift beds. It's no wonder that my subconscious throws me onto the floor at night. I wake, falling and clutching at an invisible rock-face. I am always perching on a ledge and alert to danger, even in my sleep, unless I chemically cosh myself.

Paul woke me up at midday with a cup of tea. Often, I don't know where I am, but I knew I was home. Just in a different room. Joe's room has the air of a spare, but he will be back. Georgina's will wait and wait for her to return. We leave her door propped open, so that it's still part of the family.

Monday, 29th September 2014.

At an intersection. At the motorway service station on the way to another Bereavement Break in Scotland. We queue for overpriced sustenance, although I'm not really hungry. We are glad of the distraction. Paul and I have been playing "Guess the Year" on the radio, launching into reminiscence and trying to anchor our lives in refrains and lyrics. I am officially on holiday, but I am not in the holiday mood yet. Still, we are only halfway there. Next, it is my turn to drive. I order strong coffee.

A gypsy life holds a certain appeal for me. Never stopping. Or stopping for just a while. In reality, I'd soon be found. A national alert would be issued to say that my disappearance was out of character. Maybe I'd be classed as vulnerable. People would spot me and report me, thinking that I'd thank them, one day, when I'm feeling better.

We are surrounded by slot machines: it's like eating in the middle of an amusement arcade. What is it about being on the road that makes people want to gamble? I remove the plastic dome which has seen my food safely from the servery to the checkout. I put vinegar on my jacket potato, because there's no salad cream. It tastes like vinegar and chips, without the fat or the slicing. Vinegar's okay with chips, and it's not that different. It's okay. Anything's okay in this no-person's land.

I worry whether I should have left my laptop in the car. We haven't stopped for long, but if it's stolen, all record of me will be lost. I half-hope that an opportunistic thief will have spotted it and that I'll be forced to recreate myself. There are memories that I'd like to wipe out. I want to buy a newspaper or magazine because that's what you do at service-stations, but I don't know if I've got enough focus to read a whole article.

The toilets are a disgrace, and it's another thirty-seven minutes before they're due to be re-inspected. I'm invited to have a word with the supervisor, if anything needs addressing before then. There's a blank where they're supposed to fill in the supervisor's name. I tut and I remark, loudly, but then I am on my way, without making a fuss. It's not right. It's not right at all, but it's not my problem now. I drive on, feeling disappointed with myself.

At the holiday home, we are allocated to a room which has been adapted for disabled people. It reminds me of hospitals and of the handles that Georgina needed to steady herself when she went to the loo. I have gone off into my memories of 'this time last year'.

Who has picked me up and dropped me in this alien life? I expect to wake up at any minute. It's a cliché but clichés are well-used because they ring true.

We take an evening walk along Prestwick beach, as the sun sets over Arran. I soak up the shimmering rays and warm in the ever-changing orange fire. This light captures my daughter's spirit, as far as it can be pinned down: there is an elusive quality to it. I remember how she liked to hide quietly in the dark and jump out to surprise us. There is a mischievous quality to tonight's sky.

<u>Tuesday, 30th September 2014.</u>

Our second day in Scotland. Paul and I argued our way around Prestwick this morning. It's as if remembering the time of Georgina's illness casts us back to the rows and bickering that struck us down in the hospital. The memories of that time and the realisation that this horror has really happened are making us both angry, and we have nothing to get mad at, apart from ourselves and each other. We have made up but nothing feels right. Taken away from our busy-ness with fundraising and memorials, the cracks in us and between us are turning into gaping holes. The wind whistles through, aggravating our aches and pains.

After lunch, we both fell asleep. Paul is still sleeping. He didn't want to do anything else this afternoon. I'm sitting in Arran View lounge, but I can't see Arran because of the garden wall. I can see the sky, though. Such western sky. I'm hoping it will lay on another spectacular sunset show this evening. I wonder whether to go for a walk along the beach by myself. I warned Paul that I might go out. Sometimes, I'm starting to feel I'm not safe on my own. I should make myself bear the aloneness. I spend half my life moaning that I don't have time to myself, staying up all night to claim the silence. Yet now, when I finally have the chance of solitude, it makes my heart race. Not in a good way, but like before an interview where I know I will be grilled and rejected.

My memorial fingerprint silver necklace is glinting in the afternoon light. All the mums here have a fingerprint necklace. It's a secret sign that you've lost a child, like a Christian's outline of a fish scraped in the sand. We have been skirting around the other bereaved parents with shy nods and "See you later" at mealtimes. I wish we could get straight down to the real business of comparing our respective pain and of reassuring each other that we can get through all this without going totally mad. These are the reasons I have come here, although the food and the views are also good for the soul. This is a strange kind of retreat, with children (siblings of those lost to cancer) running down the corridors and jolly Scottish lilts tinkling through the walls. There are probably lots of other sounds, but I am going deaf. ENT have confirmed it. Age-related, they think. If my deafness progresses at this rate, life will be one long silent retreat.

The clouds are racing past the bay window. To the right is north. I can hear a hum that I hope is the TV's surround sound system, rather than tinnitus. There is a smell of furniture polish and new leather sofas. The Rennie Mackintosh fireplace has been stained dark and topped with a plasma screen. Art deco/arts and crafts (I'm not quite sure of the difference) motifs repeat themselves in the cornice. Again and again – imperfect replications, like a cancer cell misprint. I can see where the plaster has been repaired. There is a flaw in this beauty, and once I've noticed it, it's all I can see. But I'm glad that they managed to save the feature at all. A Thomas Tank Engine 'Round the Rails Game' box under the armchair beneath the window reminds me that the primary purpose of this place is to let children with cancer be children.

From the emulsioned ceiling-rose, the light-fitting hangs on a silver chain, like my daughter's fingerprint. It is dangling and swaying like a fortune-teller's pendulum, even though I have never been in air with less movement.

Wednesday, 1st October 2014.

Still in Scotland. We've finally spoken to some of the other parents staying here. Some are even rawer in their grief than we are. I stay up late talking to a young mother who, like me, feels guilty, should she happen to laugh. We discuss our impatience with even the most kindly-meant platitudes – in particular, religious consolation. Like me, she thinks that people are looking at them when they go out and, like Paul, her husband says she's imagining it. We both hate being called 'hyper-sensitive'.

I have been watching the sunset show – a different variation every night. I have marched along that prom by myself and breathed saline in and out. Breathe. In and out. I mumbled to Georgina, as I sometimes do, and I noticed how the wind absorbed my voice. So I spoke louder – increased to the volume of a proper conversation.

"Goodnight, sweetheart. I love you."

I spoke clearly, as if she were in the room with me. Except I was on a windswept sea-front, rather than in a room. No matter: it did not feel like talking to myself.

<u>Thursday, 2nd October 2014.</u>

Waiting in our room, getting ready to strike out on a day trip to the Isle of Cumbrae. The house is too hot. My clothes have become unbearably heavy and I strip off as far as I dare. Nobody in here bats an eyelid, but you've got to remember to cover up and take a coat when you go outside. You can see the hills of Arran today. You can see their tops, but the light and cloud could change at any minute. I try to commit their outline to memory, just in case they're not there when I get back. I wish I knew how to draw. Sometimes, words aren't enough (or maybe I just haven't thought long and hard enough to find the right words – the ones which will encapsulate and suffice?)

We open the window, letting in the Ayrshire air. It's only a crack, because there's a restrictor on the frame, to keep us safe. We need stopping from falling out, even though we're on the ground floor and the soft surface of the children's play area is directly outside. You can't be too careful. I feel the cold air from outside collide with the inside heat – shifting around to find a way of coexisting so that hot and cold become a steady, containing, body-temperature room-temperature. I am like a fevered child, throwing off my blankets, then shivering. It would be churlish to complain when the charity is doing all this for us, so I strip and focus on keeping myself hydrated.

We catch the ferry to Cumbrae and we drive to a picnic area on the other side of the island to the main settlement. It is like a relaxation video, come to life, with the lapping of the water on the shore, and the beating of the warm, unseasonal sun through my Autumn-Winter boots. The sand here is crystalline and pink. Cerise seaweed hangs from the rocks like a snagged sweater. I step over newly opened razor shells with moist pearlescent linings. Paul is asleep on a slab of stone, high on the beach. The waves can hardly be called waves – they are folds in the water, breaking softly.

I follow the path of thick-tread footprints. Only so far – there are no other cars around and I don't know how loud I'd have to scream for Paul to stir. I identify the song of a bird that I'm pretty sure is the same as the one that chirps when I doze in my back garden. I'm pretty sure, but I'm aware that I'm going deaf. I don't wake Paul to ask him. Still asleep, Paul groans and shuffles on his back along the rusty, grey rocks, trying to find a Paul-shaped crevice. I pick up rose coloured shells and try to fix the exact shade in my mind, ready for tomorrow's manicure appointment.

Licking my finger to turn my notebook page in the breeze, it tastes of salt, like a watermelon slice bought from a beach seller at the edge of the Mediterranean. At my feet, there's a scattering of white and grey feathers that other bereaved parents might take as a 'sign'. But to me, today, this is just evidence of a scrap between gulls. It is nothing but a sure sign that things live and things die on this beach.

I dream of the necklaces I could make from my beachcombing. I'd make such a good living that I'd never have to go home. The rocks glisten as if Kelly the glitter-crazy nurse has been doing her rounds. I look for flaws in the strata and striations, guessing where they would split if I smashed stone on rock, like a child. Like a child jarping eggs at Easter, then crying when the perfect, pointy end caves in.

I want to fill my cardigan pockets with shells, stones and glass, but the pragmatic me knows we have nowhere to keep them. I am supposed to be avoiding collecting any more clutter. A splinter of red rock shatters between my fingers with the application of the lightest of pressure. It has soft, woody insides. Mustard yellow algae remind me of the colour of my fingers after I've dipped naan bread into hot, sharp pickle. Even when I scrape away the top layer of sand, using shards of quartz to comb patterns in it, there are just more crystals – ever-tinier and still opalescent – underneath. Paul is still asleep.

On the way back, we pass a Funeral Directors with a sign advertising 'Intimations'. I must find out what that means. I don't want to know what that means.

Friday, 3rd October 2014.

Last day. I dreamt that I had to tell a neighbour that one of her sons had died. Everyone was out looking for this lady, but when they found her, they all averted their gaze. I approached her and said "I think there may be some sad news for you." Everyone glared at me. The surviving son was going to beat me up, for telling her. Somebody had to tell her – a mother has a right to know.

This week has forced me to think about Georgina. People tell you to remember the happy things, but it's so painful to remember and have to force myself to believe that she's not here any more. It's almost easier to keep on going and to busy myself so that I don't have time to stop and think. But it's probably not healthy. Plus, I don't want to forget a single thing about her. I would like to keep my memories raw and fresh but it's too agonising to do that forever. There's a strong element of self-protection in my compartmentalisation.

Every fibre of me misses my daughter, but I can't function if I let this pain take over all the time. On the other hand, I need to feel it sometimes – to let it out bit by bit, so that it doesn't boil over uncontrollably.

I've been wanting to write about Georgina but I sit at my computer or with my notebook and write about everyone and everything else. Of course, she's in there, in every paragraph or scribble, because her loss is part of me, now. But I'd like to write – square-on – about who and how my daughter was. I am flinching at the word "was": maybe the difficulty is in facing up to her being in the past tense, whereas I still like to think of her as present. Albeit just out of sight, or staying over at a friend's.

I'm going to brainstorm my memories. One day soon, I'll use these notes to write an elegy:

- her cheeky smile, with a slight upturn of one side of her top lip
- the twitch in her cheeks when she was trying to keep a straight face
- her penchant for jumping out on people
- the award for 'Driest Sense of Humour' on her primary school field-trip

- honking like a goose (just because she could)
- having the conviction to laugh very loudly when she really found something funny
- her earnest face when going on stage; its gradual brightening as she relaxed into the song; the shy smile and sideways glance during the applause.

Am I already remembering photos? Am I remembering images of my daughter, rather than the real girl? She is slipping from my grasp. What do I actually recall about Georgina?

- her frail wrists. Delicate and slender. Encased in a thousand fresh and faded friendship bracelets
- her button nose, and how she hated it
- her chocolate brown eyes. How, aged eleven or so, she came out of an eye-test and told us that the optician had said she was "bong-eyed". Physically restraining her father from going in and tackling about this until she revealed it was a joke
- the phase of making stuff up for no apparent reason. Like wearing plain-glass spectacles to school and telling everyone she was short-sighted. Telling her granny "la luen" meant "the moon" in Swedish
- her graceful, swan's neck, with a biscuit-coloured stork mark at the nape
- the random clicking of her jutting hip joints as she went about her business. Who knew that Clicking Hips is a Syndrome?

- her hypermobile limbs bending at impossible angles. Making people squeal by 'straightening' her elbows way beyond 180 degrees
- the hunt for push-up bras which would make her two cup-sizes bigger. So much self-criticism, when she was so stunning
- Georgina's thunderous frown when made to do something she didn't like. The ferocity of her eyes as they darkened with displeasure
- taking her boyfriend home in the car and Georgina getting out with him to hug him goodbye. The effort of stopping myself being embarrassing or saying anything 'mother-ish' when she got back in with me
- clothes shopping. So much clothes shopping. She would want to buy everything. How I tried to be strict over skirt lengths and the showing of flesh, because she was too desperate to grow up way too fast. Now I'm glad she did at least have a taste of being a 'young adult', in some respects. If she'd remained more child-like – bided her time, as I advised – she would have missed out on even more. She did not have all the time in the world
- her vociferous insistence "I'm not a vegetarian". The rest of our nuclear family eats neither fish, flesh nor fowl, but we let her make up her own mind. She supplemented a mainly veggie diet with chicken nuggets. Nothing that looked too like the parts of a bird. She still ordered a

Happy Meal when she went to McDonalds
to see her peers and to be seen

- staying on Facebook until the early hours
of the morning and refusing to admit she
was tired, in the morning. Refusing, ever,
to admit she was tired, until those last few
months

- my daughter coming home crying because
some kids at school were being racist to a
new kid. Her shock at this encounter with
their hatred of difference. Her bravery in
challenging the culprits, even though it
made her 'different', too. We cuddled on
the sofa, and I told her that I was proud
and her anger at this injustice seeped into
me, as if by osmosis

- Georgina's inability to 'suffer fools' or hide
her dislikes. Inherited, I fear, from her
mother

- how she acted as her dad's personal
barber, following the curves of his skull
with clippers as he leant over the bath. He
did not trust me to do it, since I made him
bleed

- picking out her brother's socks, so that his
haphazard outfits might look more co-
ordinated

- refusing to do her brother's bidding, when
he tried to get her to be his slave, or offered
her two pence to fetch things for him. I was
ready to step in to stop this abuse of his
big-brother power, but I didn't need to

- the hobbies. Oh God, all those hobbies: the
ballet, the Brownies, the violin, the
performing arts, the piano, the horse-

riding. She persevered with them all, because she was not a quitter, but only the singing really stuck

- entertaining herself for hours by sketching and colouring outfits and hair do's that she had designed

- the living room corner piled with Polly Pockets and Bratz dolls and Barbies and the accessories and vehicles they needed to go on spa trips and ski trips and picnics. She acted out a thousand lives through those plastic figures: she actually lived one-fifth of her own

- spending hours on her make-up and hair, even before school, because she thought she wasn't beautiful. I assured her she was beautiful. I told her not to be vain and self-obsessed. I felt relief when she occasionally gave off a whiff of a sense of quiet satisfaction that she looked – only just-good enough

- sniffing behind her ears, which were shell-like and flush with her head, like her dad's, rather than the sticky-out wing-nuts that she could have inherited from me. Let's just say that I wear my hair long and around my face for a reason

- having play fights with her, because her dad's heart-condition made even pretend-combat risky. My ultimate weapon: my threat to sit on her and squash her

- Mum and Dad's Taxi Service being available day and night, in an attempt to let her have freedom but keep her safe

- my daughter's loyalty, and steely sense of right and wrong
- her deep, deep-thinking and questions that were too old for her years
- Georgina's sense of being in the shadow of her clever big brother's huge personality. When all the time she was a light: she was incandescent.

Monday, 13th October 2014.

I haven't been writing. I brought a bug back home with me from Scotland, and I've been bunkered down, laden with self-pity.

When I took my notebook out of my handbag today, my passport fell out with it. I had to take it with me to the hospital, when I went about my ear: they need proof that the sick are who they claim. My passport looks so important with its gilt crown and its Latin and its French. It's surprisingly light. A compact, portable passport to anywhere. People steal, lie and kill to get their hands on one of these. I'll put it away in the drawer until the next time I have to prove that I have the right to be freed of pain. Or that I am indeed the person who did 37 mph in a 30 mph zone and needs to be made more aware of their speed.

Monday, 13th October 2014.

Helen Anderson posted:
'Two Thirds of a Piece' Update
Paul and I are chuffed to bits (and a bit emotional)!

11 months ago today, a day before our beautiful daughter Georgina died, her original single 'Two Thirds of a Piece' was released. It stormed up the charts, thanks to support from Georgina's friends and well-wishers worldwide.

Having checked the relevant account today, we can confirm that an amazing sum of £6143.16 has been credited by Sony from download sales. In addition, we have received £46 in performance royalties from PPL.

Georgina was happy to know that her song would be heard, and asked for any proceeds to be split between Teenage Cancer Trust and Cancer Research UK. It is great that we will be able to forward such a substantial amount to both charities, on Georgina's behalf. Thank you to everyone who bought 'Two Thirds of a Piece' and for helping share Georgina's unique voice.

Wednesday, 22nd October 2014.

Helen Anderson posted:
Thinking of my beautiful daughter Georgina who would have been sixteen today xxxx Always remembered, always loved xxxxxx

Helen Anderson posted:
So grateful for the support of family and friends today. Thanks to everyone for their kindness xxx

Tuesday, 28th October 2014.

A school friend of Georgina's called in tonight. She was carrying two bouquets. The orange one was for us, she said. She had been thinking about us, left behind, especially on Georgina's birthday last week. The other - pink - bunch was for Georgina. She and another girl were taking it to the beach, where her ashes are scattered.

This school friend went through a phase of being unkind to my daughter, not so long ago, but she is truly sorry. She told Georgina so, when Georgina's cancer was diagnosed, and she had already said so, way before that. The dog recognises her and is totally thrilled to see her. There's something about her slight air of mischief that touches me. I remember how Georgina invited her round, when they'd made up, and how I'd said, "Let bygones be bygones." They looked blank and I had to explain the phrase. They'd squealed with laughter at my quaintness.

"Leave the past in the past. Forgive."

Sunday, 2nd November 2014.

London. I meet my son at the Victoria and Albert Museum. I love the *Horst: Photographer of Style* exhibition. Joe is so underwhelmed by the original *Vogue* covers that he doesn't even feign an interest, once he has had the pleasure of showing his new corporate hospitality pass. In the Constable show, we compare the artist's sketches to the final product. Joe likes the explanation of the way the artists used to trace outlines of landscapes onto glass. He lines it up, squinting. We wonder if this method constitutes slight cheating, like painting from a photo. We are reassured to see that the glass-tracing technique was advocated by Leonardo da Vinci.

We look for somewhere suitable for lunch. It's pouring with rain and the tourists are sheltering in South Kensington's eateries and drinkeries. Joe suggests that we dodge down into the Tube and go somewhere more central: the centre will be emptier, on a Sunday. I suspect that this has been his cunning plan, all along, because he likes to stick to familiar territory. We eat in his favourite Holborn branch of his favourite Italian restaurant chain, not far the university from which he's just graduated. We pop over the road to the "best pub in London", which is empty, but has an apparently enviable revolving menu of real ale. I drink Diet Coke, because I'm dosed up on painkillers for a dental abscess. Joe tells me to smile, and I tell him that I'm smiling inside. My face is about to throb open.

We walk to Blackfriars. He will head north to his bachelor pad, and I will head south to stay at my sister's with her Sunday-tired children on the eve of a new half-term. Joe and I stop for half a shandy at a pub he's never tried before. On his phone, he scrolls through lists of houses in the suburbs on Rightmove. I remark that he's stretching the definition of 'commutable distance'. I smile inside at the way he curls his mouth when he concentrates. My son's hair is spikey-mad, like when he was a toddler. It needs cutting, but I fear that he will take himself off for another butchers' crew-cut, if I mention the barbers again. He looks handsome, anyway, in a turquoise polo shirt. I approve, but he doesn't care diddly-squat about his appearance.

At the station, he suffers a kiss from me, before he points me in the direction of my train, He looks a bit sad as I say goodbye. I'm fairly sure I'm not imagining it. In two weeks' time, he'll travel home to 'celebrate' the anniversary of his little sister's death. He lets me hug him harder than I ever used to. To his credit, he barely even shudders.

It's been so wonderful to hear someone call me "Mum" again. It is a broad, deep, Yorkshire "Mum", unrounded and unflattened by his first weeks in a City office.

<u>Monday, 10th November 2014.</u>

Getting ready for Georgina's 'anniversary'. Some people on the internet call it an 'angelversary'. Her anniversary of getting her wings. That makes it sound too joyful. I focus on fretting over practicalities – anything to stop the horror leeching through.

Paul has been looking at photos for a slideshow. If you flick through them quickly enough on the screen, she moves. You catch her particular mannerisms. I am glad that she spent hours photographing herself. I saw it as vanity and self-absorption, but now I can see that it wasn't about looking pretty or sexy: she was exploring herself, in shadow and in light. She was trying to catch all of her angles – not just her best ones.

I am dyeing my hair in readiness for the 14th. I am worrying that I haven't got a new pink outfit, which is almost expected of me. I don't want to let my public down. I say that with my tongue firmly in my cheek, but, even so, who is the vain one now? It is better to be distracted with vanity than to ache with missing my child. I need a good cry before the anniversary, so that I can put my best face forward.

Tuesday, 11th November 2014.

Helen Anderson posted:
On Friday, it will be one year since Georgina died. We have been invited in to her school to see the many fundraising activities being carried out in Georgina's honour. Not only are Joe Henderson and the new principal having their heads shaved to raise money for the TCT and a memorial garden, but the lovely Angel is donating her long hair to the charity which provided Georgina with her fantastic wig. This promises to be an emotional day (hopefully in a good way, though) xx

Monday, 17th November 2014.

Helen Anderson posted:
Today, Paul and I have been married for exactly 24 years - not all of them easy, but I am glad that we have each other and created two wonderful children xxx

<u>Tuesday, 18th November 2014.</u>

I am still getting over the 'anniversary' 'party'. It went as well as could be expected, or possibly better.

There were queues of semi-familiar faces waiting for us to dish out balloons from the cricket club pavilion. We formed a human chain, to distribute them. The music – Georgina's music – being broadcast over the cricket pitch boomed too loud, so the steward turned it down. Then we couldn't hear Georgina's voice when it was time to let go. There was a countdown crescendo and the balloons (all shapes and sizes, including the yellow ones ordered in error instead of pink) all shot up together. They blew over the rooftops out to sea so I was glad for the marine life's sake that we'd invested in biodegradable string. The colour of the latex didn't matter one bit. The music came back on as the balloons rose beyond the (kindly donated by a local business for free) floodlights.

Two of her closest friends were sobbing uncontrollably and I hugged them and cried, too. I didn't know if they wanted to pull away. The vibrations of the girls' sobs felt real; the rest of it a film-set. Lights, camera, action. I felt like an extra – a director, at best. I don't mean that I felt fake, but not totally live, either. We were all ad-libbing a read-through of a skeleton script. We are acting out an eternal Work-In-Progress.

Inside the clubhouse, the paper table cloths and the bunting and the candles and the single rose stems I'd worried about all look as pink as they should. I thought the ambience was tasteful. There was an air of contained celebration. The slideshow was a success, thanks to the pictures taken from Georgina's laptop. I will never know whether I'd have had her blessing to show her so clearly – to reveal all these facets of her. Paul and I had to make a judgement call, as 'managers of Georgina's estate.' Likewise, we cannot know which of the hundreds of songs recorded in her bedroom best represent her musical legacy, but we whittled them down according to a crude, objective system and subjective whims to form a CD of seventeen tracks. We sought permission for press copies of the covers and added Georgina's originals. They are a limited edition, being played, now, in the bedrooms of her friends and family.

When we got home afterwards, I cried because I was slightly sozzled and also because Keri - the nurse who was with us the night Georgina died - had left a message saying she was thinking of us as she drove en-route to visiting another child. A year on, children are still dying.

There were flowers from Paediatric Oncology, which were greatly appreciated. Though I presume that they'll have been prompted by a 'bring forward' note in someone's diary, it's nice to know that they remember. It's nice to know how important it is to parents to show that the staff remember, even though Georgina wasn't the first and won't be the last.

Two of Georgina's favourite teachers threw a little 'party' in the music room for Georgina's friends after school. I worry that it might have been undignified of me to get up with these lovely ladies to sing *I Know Him So Well* in the manner of Elaine Paige and Barbara Dixon. It was always going to be fraught, the three of us spontaneously trying to rearrange a duet. One minute, I was crying and consoling a girl who was crying, and the next minute I was rocking the mike, 1980s-style. I am realising that there are no rules to this and that I can't worry about Georgina watching and approving all the time (For a start, if I worry about that, I will never have sex or go to the toilet, ever again)

Before the anni/angelversary was over, people were asking me for details of the Christmas concert. We are staggering from one date to another, setting goals to break time down into chunks. Because to look in one go at the whole, interminable period to be served is more than any of us can be expected to take in.

Joe has gone back to London. He has gone home after a few days at home here. He says he'll see me in January, if he manages not to die before then, I tell him off for being distasteful. I tell him off because he has read my thoughts and said them out loud.

I wonder if there's anything left that cannot be joked about. Paul constantly reminds us of the importance of dark humour. I agree that it helps us to survive, but I won't tempt Fate or God or Whoever's Listening by laughing at Joe's remark. When your sister is taken away in the middle of the night and your parents manage to keep going and throw parties in spite of it all (even if it is because they are trying to be brave for each other and for you and for the world), you must worry that they can't protect you, either, and that they'll pick up the pieces if you are stolen too.

Maybe Joe feels guilty for surviving – God (or Whoever) knows how guilty I feel for functioning at all. What kind of a mother can carry on without her dead child? They are talking about looking into therapy for Post-Traumatic Stress Disorder for me, but I'm not so sure about it, because I'm afraid of forgetting, as well as of remembering. I go over and over each detail. I write it down so that I don't have to keep it in my head. Yet it's like a 'to do' list in the bottom of my handbag that I just have to keep checking, even though I tell myself over and over that nothing has appeared on it during the ten minutes since I last looked. I find that the fretting – the replaying – fills a space. This is how I kill time.

Saturday, 29th November 2014.

Two sleepless nights, now. Truly sleepless. I don't know if I'm not sleeping because I'm ill or feel ill because I'm not sleeping. Last night I took an extra sleeping pill, but it just laughed in my face. I am downstairs at six in the morning. It reminds me of being up in the night with Georgina. It reminds me of being up with a newborn baby, but it's lonelier and less purposeful.

How quickly my confidence in my recovery from depression falls apart, after only two sleepless nights. Madness flashes at the edge of my vision. In the darkness, shapes poke out of my wardrobe, and I clutch onto a sleeping Paul, though I know it's not fair to wake him. But if I don't hold on, I'll spin off the bed: my mind wants to leave my body, and vice versa.

All the time, I'm telling myself I'm coming down with the flu. A chemical imbalance, maybe.

Stress - I've so much to do. I cannot afford this dip right now, because I've so much to do. I cannot afford it, ever again.

On the first night of insomnia, I shifted into Joe's room. I inhaled his pillows and clung tight to his old teddy. It helped stave off the darkness, but my heart beat faster and faster. I spent hours trying to decide if I was a complete hypochondriac, or having a major medical alert. Anxiety, probably. Real physical effects brought on by an overactive mind.

Last night, I was too hot, then too cold. The pillows were too lumpy, then too fluffy. The room was not quite dark enough, so that flashes of streetlight through the curtains fed my imagination and prodded me awake. I lay there, fearing a sharp descent. I hope that it is the flu, and that it will pass quickly, this time.

Sunday, 30th November 2014.

I go Christmas shopping with my mum. Paul and I are opting out of Christmas again, this year, apart from giving cash to our nieces and nephews. My mum is opting in, and I try to get her to focus on her shopping list. Neither of us is quite sure what she is looking for.

I try to summon up even the faintest of interest in the festivities. This must be how Jehovah's Witnesses feel when the Christmas decorations go up. I have resolved to start all-new Christmas traditions, but I can't even buy in to the most muted of celebrations. I wonder how early in the autumn I'd have had to have gone away, to avoid all mention of Christmas.

I don't want to be a misery: I would like to participate at my own level, but I don't want to be shoved into it. I tell myself that I will refuse to be bullied, but I feel like an introverted five year-old knowing she's going to have to go to school and stand up for herself. I am determined. Nevertheless, I dread it.

Monday, 1st December 2014.

Waiting for my GP to phone me back after morning surgery. I have rehearsed what I'm going to say to her to the point of ravelling myself into unintelligibility. I only asked the doctor for a telephone conversation because I can't procure an appointment to see her in person. She'll probably still need to see me in the flesh, anyway. The dog is still waiting for his morning walk, because I daren't leave the house and miss catching the doctor. He's given up on it.

At what point do you chase the doctor up, in case you've been forgotten by the system? It is so agonising to be ignored and disregarded. I try to keep it in perspective: I am not dying (that I know of) and I've waited this long, so I can surely wait longer. I am getting better at the waiting and at the perspective, but my nerves still jangle. I like to know.

It's the first day of December and we have a single Christmas card on the mantelpiece. I need to hunt out my string of fairy lights for the fireplace; the vintage festive Italian postcard; the Russian tree-doll my mum brought me back from St. Petersburg. These are our new, post-Georgina Christmas decorations. Will I ever feel able to delve into the boxes of family Christmases Past that are shut away in the loft? I do not feel ready, yet, to face the decorations that she made at nursery school. But I know that I will always keep them and I will know that they are there.

Friday, 12th December 2014.

Helen Anderson posted:
Hoping as many people as possible can join us at St Mark's Church, Marske, tonight for a relaxed, Christmassy celebration of Georgina's life. 7.30 p.m. kick-off. Some tickets are available on the door so bring a friend xx

Wednesday, 17th December 2014.

Landed in Tenerife yesterday. Paul and I are here for Christmas and New Year because Joe didn't want to come home and we didn't want to go through the motions of Christmas with just the two of us in that house so laden with Christmas memories.

Last night, Paul and I sat on the balcony and discussed God (and the likely lack thereof). Then we discussed Georgina's talent and Georgina's bravery. We discussed the importance of telling her story. A news agency contacted us a few days ago about being featured in women's magazines. Thanks but no thanks. I would rather be in control of my own words and I am aware that I can only write my own story. I can't claim to know how Georgina thought and felt.

Last night, I dreamt that Georgina was an egg. I dropped her on the road. People were laughing at me for trying to scoop up the pieces, but I scraped them into a skillet, picking out the grit. Someone brought me a stretcher, but I wanted to use my own pan.

I dreamt that, in A&E, they didn't take us seriously. They kept us waiting. And then we were in a cubicle and the egg set into an omelette in the shape of a Georgina-face. As her features emerged, her eyeballs shifted from side to side. She and I said "Humpty Dumpty" in unison. I was happy, then, because I knew it was definitely her and although the omelette turned back into mush, we had proof that she was still with us because it was so typical of her to joke and diffuse the situation. We had hope that she might appear to us again.

This morning, when I told Paul about this dream, it made him very sad. He did not like thinking of his daughter as an omelette. No, not at all.

Saturday, 20th December 2014.

Today has been a good day. I got up late and ambled down to a café with panoramic views for a drink. Then, tapas by the marina. Solid sunshine. Sunbathing on the terrace, while Paul dozed.

But... the unease. I'd like to take a tranquiliser, but I can't possibly justify it. I feel as though I'm hiding out – waiting to be discovered (and not in a good way, like someone entering a talent contest, but rather that I'm about to be unmasked and exposed). I am worried because we haven't told the couple in the neighbouring apartment about our children. They have mentioned their son several times already, but we haven't even shared that we, too, have a boy back in the UK. Or that, until not so very long ago, we had a daughter, too. Being on holiday on our own – even though Joe definitely didn't want to come with us and said he wasn't planning going home for Christmas – feels like I'm denying the true shape of our family.

We know all about next door's. They, too, are here on their own. No grandchildren. Their son son's a bugger, always telling them it's nice weather at home, even when it's snowing. They used to live out in the country, but now they've got a bungalow on an estate. They've never thought of it as 'home'. We smile politely and silently. The lady next-door gives up for a while, then sticks her head back over the wall that divides our balconies. She spots that Paul is painting. The man who owns the apartment we're in paints, too, but he's rubbish. She can't see very well now (she warns us not to get old) but he doesn't get his perspectives right.

I comment that it's interesting to rent a property and guess what the owners are like from their books and belongings, but her attention is wandering. She doesn't want her monologue converted into dialogue. With any luck, we might get through four weeks without having to divulge any history. Most of the owners have gone home for Christmas, as they all have grandkids. She reiterates that she does not. Her daughter is selfish, spending every last penny on travel, and always long-haul.

Monday, 22nd December 2014.

A noticeable influx of children, now that the school holidays have started. I watch them trail around, not quite fitting in with their families. By rights, we should still be hulking around a sulky teenager. We don't belong to the elderly ex-pat demographic, but we are way past the buggies and the sunhats and the Peppa Pig rucksacks stage. The lady staying next-door has been charged with watering everybody else's plants, because most of the residents have gone home to England, to see their grandchildren's faces on Christmas morning.

There are strict rules to living in this block. The Rules of Communal Living are posted on the cork notice board in our borrowed kitchen. I have studied them, and was pleased to find that I was fully complying. Then, I found that I'd missed a second page, pinned under the numbers for Takeaway Indian and English-speaking Dentist. Now, I am worried that my shoes are not soft-soled enough, so I slide around in bare feet because I can't risk infringing the 'No clomping' rule.

I stay outside late, listening to the waves and the Englishmen in the pub. They are enjoying themselves, if their volume is anything to go by. I am adjusting to the noise, with the help of Vino De Calidad De Las Islas Canarias. When I was fifteen, I took a tourists' Spanish course which gives me a false sense of confidence when letting such strange words roll off my tongue. I look down and catch a glimpse of long, candy pink, holiday fingernails. They are similar to my daughter's but attached to my hands, which are sun-spotted with wrinkles that she'll never have the need or the chance to worry about.

Last night, we got "smashed" on half a bottle of wine, and two honey-rum shots. We were tucked up in bed by nine o'clock. The ceiling fan was spinning, even though it wasn't. We were very quiet.

Tuesday, 23rd December 2014.

We walk to the next cove and sit awhile, watching Russian children jump in the waves. Worrying about undercurrents I don't even know are there. The children have white-blonde hair. I worry about their sun protection. The mother hasn't brought hats, or has forgotten to plonk them on their heads, because she is too busy tanning and smoking. The father's in charge of two girls in the water. The older one keeps diving under the surface and I know she's doing it on purpose but it makes me anxious because the father's not timing her. I feel sick when she beats her personal record for staying submerged. The father's eyes are on the little one, but the big one's drifting away. She looks muscular and tough, but I look around for a lifebelt. The case where the lifebelt should be is hanging open – empty. I consider what else we could throw, if the waves carry her out.

I feel furious with the mother for being able to lie there, trusting that no harm will come to them. I despise her for not caring about passive smoking (she may be outside, but how many feet away is the baby in the buggy?) I wonder whether she gave up smoking during her pregnancies. Didn't she love her babies enough to stay stopped? I hate myself for being so judgmental. Grief is making me bitter.

Wednesday, 24th December 2014.

Helen Anderson posted:
Feeling slightly festive now. Thanks for all the supportive messages xxxxx

Wednesday, 24th December 2014.

The lady next-door mentions Santa. She asks if we have family and I own up to having a son. It's the truth, but not the whole truth. I stress that we wanted to spend Christmas with him, and that he's being well looked after at my sister's house.

Thursday, 25th December 2014.

Helen Anderson posted:
Warmest Christmas greetings to all my friends and family. Thanks to my sister for looking after Joe and Mum so ably xxxxx thinking of my beautiful Georgina, as always, but knowing she would want everyone to enjoy themselves xxxxxx Happy Christmas! Xxxx

Thursday, 25th December 2014.

Christmas in Tenerife. We've been here for nine days and, overall, it feels like it was a good decision. I miss Joe, although it's a relief that he's being looked after at my sister's house in London. I miss Georgina.

We went down to the marina and stood away from other people on the jetty. I played *Two Thirds of a Piece* on my iPhone and it felt as though a bit of Georgina had travelled with us. I'm glad that we still have her voice, even though she can't say anything new. We had coffee and I logged into Facebook on the café's internet, using Georgina's mini iPad. Its pink leather cover shouts "hospital" to me, because it was always at her bedside.

Lots of Georgina's friends had sent us messages. It was beautiful to know that she's not forgotten, even amidst the excitement of their family celebrations and their parties and presents. I am touched at how many of them took the time and trouble to contact us. I felt a bit of a fraud, when so many of them don't know we're away. We didn't advertise it on social media, because of the threat of being burgled – dead daughter or not. So, many of them are imagining us sitting – sad – at home. I AM sad, but in the sun.

Last year, we didn't 'do' Christmas at all, but last night we went to an ex-pats' bistro, where they have decorations and the singer was all full of mistletoe and wine. It felt okay. This morning, Paul and I exchanged one present each. We actually said "Happy Christmas", which we couldn't even bring ourselves to utter last year. We had omelette (no Georgina-faces) and chips in a local restaurant for our Christmas dinner. I admired the poinsettias in tubs on the terrace.

Now, I'm sunbathing on the balcony and Paul's dozing in the bedroom. Things could be worse, but I don't think I'll ever be properly happy again. I am focusing on 'getting by' and 'getting through' – they are achievements in themselves. When will it all seem real? I wonder if the medication I was already taking for depression and anxiety are stopping it from sinking in. I won't stop taking the tablets – I don't think I could face a more direct onslaught of emotion. Even though they may be numbed, my feelings are enough to cope with. Sometimes (only sometimes) I really want to feel the hurt I know is there. Mostly, like today, I muddle through, grateful for the anaesthetic.

Friday, 26th December 2014.

I'm alone on our balcony under a dark sky. The moon is a white crescent – a quarter moon, stranded on its back, like an overturned terrapin. By the yellow outside light, I notice that we have forgotten to water the geraniums, just as I forget, at home, after the novelty of the first few post-planting days. I must try to save them, tomorrow. I listen to the rumble and whine of our dishwasher – switched on minutes too late to comply with the building's electrical appliance curfew. Whoops.

I scratch in my notebook with my propelling pencil and families walk past, not realising I'm here. Snatches of their festive conversations wash over me without my registering which language they're speaking. The big hotel in the resort twinkles like a cruise ship. There is a flash from a balcony box – a five-star distress signal. I worry that the hotel is listing. I focus on the bursts of sax music carried to me on the breeze. At school, I passed Grade 5 Tenor Saxophone. How long would I need to practise, to become good enough to eke out a living from music, like the busker who sits by the ex-pat bar, not really playing his guitar?

I wonder what the busker's running from. Everybody here is running from something. Even those, like us, who're running, tied to a partner in a bizarre three-legged race. Racing for life. Racing against time and the winter. A street-seller tries to hawk flashing Santa hats. It is Boxing Day; does he know that his days are numbered? He must plan on staying here for a bit – I saw him picking out smart trousers in the charity shop run by the mad British dog-ladies.

The night is cold on my sun-scorched skin. A motor boat chugs on a sea which is otherwise silent. This is the life. But what life? Whose life? A white light sparkles in the black sky/sea/sky like a determined, demented firefly.

Today, we went on an excursion to La Gomera. I would have loved to have stayed on the undeveloped island overnight, in a tiny pension with dark wood shutters and a dark tiled floor and a piano in that courtyard which was just begging to be peered into. I imagine the last ferry leaving, and being stuck there with the navy blue-clad widows, and the youths whizzing around the plaza in fits of machismo. I imagine sitting on a wooden balcony against a peeling blue wall, ignoring the smell of bitter coffee and pine detergent, to roll a tot of palm honey rum around my tongue.

There is chattering from the apartment above me. A strange fusion of Cockney vowels and Spanish lisps. Maybe the New Year's crowd that the lady next-door warned us about has arrived. Last year, their noise was unbearable, she says. Her fear is seeping into me: I must resist it. Maybe all the Brits who went home to see their grandchildren for Christmas have had enough of them and sneaked back.

Wednesday, 31st December 2014.

I am alone on the coastal path near the Fisherman's Beach. I am alone, but for the beating sun and the glistening, wind-crumpled sea and the bobbing, white boats. Occasionally, a couple will walk past, but there is real quiet in between these interludes. Paul is back at the apartment. He is tired.

This morning, we went to Playa San Juan for the market, and there was already an air of fiesta about the place. It made me feel grumpy. My grumpiness wasn't helped by my toothache. Maybe I'm somatising. What's to celebrate? Getting through a year that my daughter didn't even get a grab at? I feel I've betrayed her, by getting though another year without her. I don't know if I can make it through another one. All that effort, all over again. This year, Georgina's friends will have prom and some will learn to drive. It doesn't bear thinking about. I'm finding that looking back is too sad but looking forward is impossible. So, I'm stuck in this moment, which isn't so terrible, with its sun and its sea and its silence. It's just the emptiness, especially when everyone else's happiness is about to spill over (I know – not everyone will really be happy, but it's the official, outward, public mood).

I mustn't forget the child that I still have – he is a child to be celebrated. I don't even know what he is doing, this New Year's Eve. Last year, he sat at home with me, and we did nothing much. To us, it felt like the only option, but Paul wanted to get out and be among people, so he went to the local with his best mate, Big Paul. I kept Joe close, and I wrote a list of things to focus on, such as holiday ideas and visits to long-lost friends – little milestones to reach. Perhaps I need to do the same today. Perhaps I will always need to make sure that there are punctuation points on my calendar, so that I can get through. It just makes me so angry that people don't realise that the world has stopped turning.

I love you, Georgina.

I need to phone Joe, urgently. His dad makes a point of keeping in regular touch with him – a direct message here and a text there - but I am busy being so careful not to stifle him that he must sometimes wonder whether I'm here at all. Joe brushes off my "I love you" as if I am an irritation or an embarrassment. I like to think that he likes me to say that, really. I was proud to hear that he'd been a big help at my sister's house on Christmas Day. Such a help – both my mum and my sister reported back to me that my son is a thoughtful man. I am bursting with something approximating happiness about this. I don't think I'll ever be truly, truly happy again, now that I've lost Georgina, but my son is more than enough reason to go on.

It is too quiet for Paul here, among the elderly ex-pats. He's not good at introspection. He needs a role – business and busy-ness. I am not enough for him. I wonder if he needs others to bounce off. To confirm that he's real. He can't sleep at night, here. He can't even sleep during the day, whereas he's normally a resolute dozer. He seems down, yet he larks about and it irritates me because it feels hollow and the switch from one to another doesn't quite ring true. He needs me, too. He needs me to need him and that isn't a bad thing, because I do. My tooth aches. It is a constant, just-there throb, with an occasional sharp pang. I jump out of my skin when I try to bite on it.

From my seat on the coastal path, I feel rootless and disconnected from all these strangers packed into a single, rocky cove. They remind me of battery hens, being let out for their annual run around. The flights go in and out, overhead, and we try not to catch the eye of those trundling their suitcases to the coach pick-up point. Among this temporary accommodation – this lack of belonging – I have found my place. I fear that Paul has not.

Back at the apartment, as all the languages and the holidaymakers' emotional Esperanto drift past our balcony, I let the foreignness flow over me. I am at ease with this transience. I wish that this eternal motion could be captured and taken home with me.

A thunderstorm breaks out, and I retire indoors to listen to the rain slosh around on the tiled terrace. At first, I thought that the lightning was our neighbours taking flash photographs. I was tutting at them dragging their furniture across the floor, when, all the time, it was thunder. It was a relief not to have to feel angry with them. I didn't mind the disturbance when I found out that nature was behind it. Nature has the right to shake me up a little, every now and again.

Thursday, 1st January 2015.

There is still that childish delight in writing out the New Year's date for the first time. Like when you're at primary school and the teacher chalks the date on the blackboard on the first day back after the Christmas holidays.

Last night, Paul and I went for a meal at a little Spanish restaurant and we listened to the ex-pats on the neighbouring tables competing for the Who's Lived Here Longest? Prize. There were hordes of them, trying to distinguish themselves from temporary tourists. I thought I might like to live out here in the sun, but I don't want to be part of that set: this much I have decided.

There was a dance in the village square, and I couldn't take my eyes off a little girl in a red dress, with flicked-out, honey-brown hair. Aged about two, she was so serious in her quest for fun. So watchful of the older girls, who were teaching her how to party right.

We went back to our apartment before midnight, partly because there were no seats left, and partly because the public display of happiness was a little hard to bear. We sat on the balcony, wearing the silly hats we had been given at the restaurant. We watched the sky – first lanterns, then fireworks from the big hotels to our left and to our right. Like a pyrotechnic tennis match or poetry slam. This year, we managed to wish each other a Happy New Year.

Friday, 2nd January 2015.

I have come up with an idea for a second novel. So far, it is not earth-shattering, plot-wise, but I think I can do its subject-matter justice. It will be about grief; how the loss of a child reshapes a family; how differently a bereaved mother and father react; what happens to the sibling left behind. The characters are taking shape – they are like us, but they are not us – and I have enough of a storyline to begin. I may eventually follow a very different path to the one I'm envisaging now. Fluidity, I have learned, is key.

I'm just about ready to start typing up my fiction. It's coming from an authentic place, and I believe in it. Yet, part of me's protesting that I should also write my 'fact' – that I should type up these diaries , straight and direct, before I go around the houses and fictionalise my own story. I have a strong urge to face this thing head-on. I want to deal in the real and the actual. But I don't know if I can trust my feelings and I don't know whether I can trust my writing.

So far, therapeutically speaking, my writing hasn't let me down. I just don't know if anyone will want to read what I've got to say. There's been a mixed response to my attempts to secure an agent for my first novel. First, there was some interest, then some wavering, then a rattle of rejections and half-compliments and a deathly hush. I try to laugh it off, this nibbling at my confidence. Maybe one day I'll paper the walls of my new mansion with those rejection letters. How I'll laugh. Or maybe not.

But this feels like a real case of something needing to be written. It's almost as though not writing up my true story (I say "my" because I'm acutely aware that I can't claim to be able to author Georgina's) would be a betrayal. I am also aware that that sounds pretentious, but I stand by it. I have just read Marion Coutts' *Iceberg: A Memoir* about caring for her brain tumour-ridden husband and raising a two-year-old. It was not light holiday reading. I would be proud to write something as honest as that painful book.

Tuesday, 6th January 2015.

A difficult night, last night. Desperately missing my daughter. I lay awake, with my heart thumping through my ear onto the pillow. Tears formed in the corners of my eyes, but they stuck there, lumpen, just like me. I was selfishly glad when Paul finally indicated that he was also awake. We talked through our maddest, most unspeakable thoughts: our jealousy of the parents whose children were enjoying the 'Coming of the Kings' parade in the village. And our worse jealousy – an outrage on Georgina's behalf - towards their living, breathing little ones. We talked about the strangeness of being out here on an extended not-quite-holiday. It's calming for me to be away from questions and remarks and memories of Georgina. I think that I needed this space, but my mind is turning back to her, now that we are going home.

What is clear is that Paul can't cope without having a pet project. He is a man who needs Something To Do. Right before we came away, we had a concert to organise. Next, a mad few days of frantic packing. But now, when it is still, it doesn't suit him at all. His soul is twitching, along with his restless legs.

He worries that people are getting on with their lives and forgetting her, although that's also what he wants for them. I hope he doesn't think I'm forgetting her, too. I'm clinging to my writing and punctuating my diary with trips and treats, to confirm to myself that I am going to continue continuing – to commit to a life that I don't really want because it would be an insult to Georgina to waste it, since I have the chance of it (at least, for now). I never, ever forget Georgina. She is an ache in my breastbone: a joyous pang that I don't want to quell.

Watching the Spanish children celebrating with their families brought back memories of all the Euro-pop we have danced to together, on package holidays; of little Georgina's joy in swishing the skirts of floaty sundresses and twirling on polished wooden dance floors. She was such an adorable dot, with her bunches held by flowery bobbles. She liked strappy, shimmery sandals, or clompy pink trainers with lights in the soles that flashed as she stamped her feet.

Of course, I remember her temper tantrums, too – they'd have been a lot less frustrating, all-round, if we'd known then about her being on the autistic spectrum. We only had an ASD diagnosis for her in the last year or so of her life, having been assured when she was three years old by a panel of experts that she was not affected by this particular gene which impacts upon many of her relatives. That she was just struggling to cope with my own depression and other family dynamics. I regret the missed chances to help her with her difficulties in adjusting to change. I regret telling her to control herself – in effect, telling her to not be herself – when this was actually beyond her. I felt as though she was defying me and expressing her resentment of me. And it is true that she had an iron will. But there was no malice in it – she was pre-programmed to need to stick to a plan and to see things, clearly, as black-or-white.

It seems strange that the few people we've met here don't know about our tragedy. I feel that my sadness oozes from my pores but they're too absorbed in their own worlds to notice, or too polite to mention it. I find it liberating not to have to go over it with people who don't understand. I know that it happened. When we go home, we will have to find a new kind of 'normal', where Georgina is still part of the family, but where she is not the whole focus as she has been (quite rightly so) for these last eighteen months. I need to stop hiding away from people and to make some decisions about my focus and direction.

Paul, in my opinion, needs to work out how to keep himself busy, to a healthy degree. We need to find a new balance point, in these storms. For me, it will be building in these quiet, undisturbed periods. For Paul, I hope it will be dotting his too-quiet days with people-filled outings and new things to stop him getting stuck.

We are not yet fifty years old. Nobody knows how long they've got left on this planet, but we could have twenty to thirty years ahead, and I can't say I'm winding my life down. Not just yet. Being among all these elderly English-folk-abroad has shown me that we haven't quite reached that stage, yet. We don't quite fit in to the retirement-to-the-sun scene, although it looks to be a pleasant one.

This month has been a productive one for me, writing-wise – and a calm one, emotionally – so I would do it all over again. I would like to replicate this time away, in the future. But whether it would be good for Paul to be still and alone (except for my company) again for so long, any time soon, is another matter.

<u>Friday, 9th January 2015.</u>

Four nights and three days to go. I am savouring these last moments of isolation. I have been easing myself back onto Facebook. Paul has spent a small fortune on data so that he can roam the internet, and I have been known to piggyback on paulhotspot, from time to time. I haven't dwelt too long among the rants about snow and planning applications. I have just dipped in for long enough to establish a brief reconnection with home.

I told the elderly couple staying in the apartment next door about Georgina, the other day, when we were gossiping over the balcony wall. I could sense that they were about to tell me that boys were easier to raise, and that I am lucky to only have a son. I could see where the conversation was going, but I failed to see a way to head it off. In the end, it wasn't so bad, telling them my situation. Mainly, I felt desperate to reassure them that they hadn't upset me (they hadn't – not any more than I was already upset).

Later on, they were talking about wheelchairs and I realised that I was contributing to the discussion as if I had no personal experience of access issues, when, in fact, I had had to negotiate a steep learning curve in this respect, when chemo destroyed the nerves in Georgina's feet. I keep finding myself feeling sorry for people in unfortunate situations – not allowing myself to admit that I, too, am a person to be pitied. I don't know if I'm in denial, or if it's a case of refusing to be defined by tragedy.

Paul and I went for a walk, and sipped two long coffees at the café on the headland. We talked about the things we might like to do this year. We set some goals – big ones and little ones. Last year, it helped me to make a list, so we wrote down the names of people we might visit, and ideas for celebrating our silver wedding anniversary. We listed changes we might make to our house, and trips we might take, so that we can refer to it when we feel overwhelmed by grey sameness, or find ourselves at an inevitable impasse.

I'm concerned that many of my ideas involve getting away – I need to furnish my life so that it is comfortable enough to inhabit every day, rather than only on 'high days' and holidays. I need to include little motifs like playing badminton and going to antique sales. Maybe I could start to run classes or be more involved with writing groups, again. I need to syncopate my life with little 'tings' of a silver triangle, as well as with great big clangs of cymbals.

Together, we came up with an adequate-enough list-of-sorts. Now I just need to hold on to this sense of... I was going to say "purpose", but it is not quite that definite. Equally, "hope" is too committed. Maybe I mean "possibility". There is a faint – but real – whiff of possibility.

Sunday, 11th January 2015.

How quickly the sun drops, at this time of year, even out here. From oven to fridge in minutes. I am probably exaggerating: cold is relative. Next week, I'll remember what real cold is. North-East English cold - more than the need to pull a cover-up over your swimsuit. It's almost time to go home and I realise I've failed to water the indoor and outdoor plants, as requested by their absent owner. We have two days to bring them back to life before we leave them out here for the rest of the Canarian winter. They will be at the mercy of the elements, if he does not hurry back from his family. Even so, they may fare better than they have done under our care. Tomorrow, I will soak them, but it may be too late.

Wednesday, 14th January 2015.

We come home to a Christmas card from the old university friend that I forgot to tell about Georgina, last year. I have still forgotten to tell her and she includes Georgina's name. It's quite nice to see my youngest included in the good wishes.

Wednesday, 14th January 2015.

Helen Anderson posted:
Home - safe and sound, and unlikely to come out from under this blanket for some time. I only like my snow far up volcanoes, and well away from me!

Friday, 16th January 2015.

Helen Anderson posted:
A lovely post-holiday surprise for us at the Mermaid pub quiz last night:
Thanks to Pauline Richmond and all the Mermaid Quiz regulars for the donation of £1000 of raffle proceeds to a charity in memory of Georgina. We'd like the money to support The Sick Children's Trust's home-from-home for families of seriously ill children at the RVI Newcastle, as we've seen how important it is for parents from all over the region to have a base close to their sick child. We told the home's manager this morning and she was as thrilled as we were. We have some great friends and neighbours in Marske xxx (and no, we didn't win but it didn't matter!)

Friday, 23rd January 2015.

Just back from London. At Joe's request, I went to be on hand while he went through dental surgery. He took it in his stride, so we had a mother-son sightseeing weekend, instead. So strange to be a mum again, for the weekend. I worry that he's not eating healthily or that he'll get knocked over. I'm not too keen on the proximity of his offices to the Stock Exchange, which surely must be a terrorist target. I wish that they would reinstate the abandoned check-points from IRA days, with immediate effect. I need to keep my boy protected.

I think about my own years as a London civil servant, a few streets away from mortar attacks on Downing Street. I remember being advised to crouch under my desk while an abandoned car with a suitcase on the back seat was blown up by the Army outside our office. We put a lot of trust in those special blinds which were meant to catch any stray shards of reinforced glass. I remember lying in bed at night and hearing the thud of bombs at Arnos Grove Underground and under a bridge on the North Circular. My mum said nothing about fear, though all three of her children journeyed around that threatened city, day in and day out.

I feel an unreasonable annoyance with Joe for being reckless (eating and drinking the wrong things; not paying proper attention to the traffic) with this life that he has, when his sister has none. But recklessness is normal for one who is still so young. I have to let him be young. I must stop calling him "Baby", especially in public.

I have an ache – almost a lump – somewhere between my intestines and the void where my womb used to be. A phantom tumour in my liver? An actual tumour? It will no more go away with a bit of positive thinking than an antacid could have dealt with Georgina's mutating cells.

Someone phoned Paul to ask how we are, which was nice. She told him that she's heard we'll feel better when we hit the two year mark. Definitely. That's what's she's been told. Paul doesn't swear until he puts the receiver down. Such control.

Saturday, 7th February 2015.

These last few weeks have been dark and cold. I make arrangements with people, then immediately regret committing myself. Then, I force myself to stick to them. I think that it's good for me to force myself beyond my comfort zone but it also leaves me in a state of panic. When do you know when to push yourself? When is enough enough?

I have been committing these diaries of mine to my computer hard drive. At first, it felt like a relief: like something I was meant to do. But it's painful to go over those early days (God knows, it's still 'early days') and I wonder if it's the reason that I haven't been sleeping. I don't cope well when I don't sleep. I don't cope well with lying there at 4 a.m., trying to cling on to Paul without waking him up; with my yearning for my lost girl; with the fear of forgetting how it feels to have her lying next to me; or the pain of remembering.

We went out for coffee with Chloe this week, and I switched back into 'mum of teenage daughter' mode. I wanted to scoop her up and protect her and have humorous banter. I wanted to discuss hairstyles and who might be talking to whom. I miss that chatter. But even if I saw Chloe every day, it wouldn't dull this pain of losing my very own, very particular teenage girl. She was a one-off and she was mine – but not for long enough. Spending time with Chloe made me miss Georgina even more. It was as if she had been brought tantalisingly near.

We also went into school to discuss the memorial garden that they are planning. The smell of the dinner hall reminded me of the smell that used to cling to Georgina's blazer. The school has formally been taken over by a chain of academies, so her friends have all been issued with black blazers with a different badge. Things have changed. It saves me the pain of seeing the flashes of the old bright blue jackets passing by our lounge window. But it brings home how the world has already moved on, without my daughter.

I am further and further away from her. Yet, when I drive past the school, I still think that she might be in there. I sometimes wonder what time she is due to finish. By the time that the garden is finished, Georgina's friends will have left, and Georgina would no longer have been at school, if she had lived.

Her friends tweet and post on Facebook about college applications and mock exam results. My friends bemoan the difficulties of shopping for prom dresses. Such trials. What a nice difficulty to have #firstworldproblems #alivechildproblems. I have to force myself not to make bitter comments. It's not their fault. It's nobody's fault.

At 4 a.m., it's time for my crying. Sometimes, Paul senses it in his sleep and reaches out to me. But I don't wake him and by morning he has no recollection of my distress.

I have had another birthday. Fewer people remembered it than last year. It's commonly held that the first year is the hardest, and they might well believe that. So they might have presumed that my second birthday without Georgina would be so much easier that they need not make such a big deal of it and of my feelings. In many ways, that's what I want – some kind of normality. I want things to go back to how they were, but we are all irrevocably changed, and that is not going to happen. I need to know that Georgina isn't forgotten. I am torn between wanting friends to move on with their lives, and wanting time to be frozen.

I have taken up playing badminton with my friend Rachael. I have spoken to my friend Joan about helping her out with teaching creative writing. She is busy at the moment, but it's in the pipeline. I have signed up for a therapeutic writing course that is starting locally in March. I am going through the motions. I am told that I'm doing well and I agree because, objectively, it is true enough. But before I've finished nodding my head, I've already thought "Well, I can always drive into the sea on the way home." Although I don't really intend to, the thought is a comfort.

It's a tiny comfort at 4 a.m. and several times a day.

I play Georgina's CD over and over, as I drive in my car. I sing along, devising my own harmonies. Sometimes, they work. Other times, they jar, but I enjoy the togetherness of our duet.

Tuesday, 10th February 2015.

Helen Anderson posted:
If only Paul Anderson would buy me a little cottage in Tenerife, I would be soooooo smiley all the time. And he could have naps.

Thursday, 19th February 2015.

Helen Anderson posted:
Feeling so blah today. I'm missing my daughter so much, and even things like going round Tesco are fraught with extra sadness, as I see all the kids on half-term, and I'm not buying any teenager-food.

Monday, 23rd February 2015.

We have come away to the fishing village of Staithes. We are always coming away, so that we don't come apart. It's so hard being in our house, with just us and the dog in it. I feel as if that house is pressing down on me. Here, I am hoping for peace and quiet, in which to write. I am hoping to base the setting of my next novel on this unique place.

Last week, I had a meltdown. I came undone. It was my trip round Tesco that did it –

seeing so many kids on half-term holidays, and all the teenager-food like pizza and crisps at knockdown prices. I thought I was going to explode with the misery. I managed to get myself home, in one piece.

Then, I lay on Georgina's bed in her room upstairs – her real bedroom – for the first time since I lay there next to her while she slept off her chemo. I remember how she woke up, hours later, and she couldn't believe I was still there. I wouldn't have moved for anything. She hadn't been given the final, worst news yet, but I already had a sense that I was making memories.

This time, I cuddled her pillow and a solitary cuddly toy. The tears came and I felt so awful that I nearly stopped them. But I let them come. Paul came home to find me, mascara-smudged, in our daughter's bedroom. This is a place where I've feared to tread. We talked about our loss. We agreed that it isn't fair. We both feel so ANGRY for Georgina, who had her future snatched away.

I plonked a slightly (i.e. very) self-indulgent post on Facebook about how miserable I felt. About the yearning for my girl. I don't often post on there about my feelings but I needed the sympathy. The sympathy came rushing in. It was a bit (i.e. a lot) selfish of me because I knew that I'd worry people. But some folk seem to have been bleating on about inconsequential worries and petty slights and the cost of prom dresses, and I have felt that they are quickly forgetting the new sense of perspective that they said Georgina's illness and death gave them. It was one good thing that came out of the shortness of her life – our friends' and complete strangers' realisation that the small stuff is not worth sweating. And now they are forgetting that, so soon. Are they forgetting her? I could not stand that.

My neighbour Jackie came round with flowers: I felt cared for, and I felt guilty. I do want people to get on with their lives – what is the alternative? Stopping their lives, too, would be a waste of this amazing opportunity they've been given to carry on breathing. But I want them to show that they know that they are lucky. I want them to hold tight to that sense of gratitude and appreciation of life. And I want them to show that they are remembering Georgina, from time to time, as they go through their life and she is not able to go alongside them.

I want people to remember her on the big days and on the small days. I want to know that people know that she was on this earth. My daughter lived. So many wants – I sound like a foot-stamping toddler. I could easily find it in myself to lie on the floor and kick and hold my breath until I am blue.

We are on our fourth night of this holiday in Staithes, in a rickety old cottage which has a cubby-hole for a kitchen and amazing views over the tidal beck and the pantile rooftops and the wooden footbridge. Mainly, it has been sunny, but we've had the coal fire burning. The dog is very afraid of its crackling noise, so this evening I've opted to feel chilly instead.

I have taken lots of photos to act as a reference for the physical setting of my new novel. I have started writing up my notes and hoping that it will all come out in the wash, in some kind of book-shaped form. I wonder if I am kidding myself: if so, it is a pleasurable delusion as I sit on the wintry beach and sup drinks in the Cod and Lobster, all in the name of research.

We've met up with Donna, Georgina's school music teacher, who has been amazingly supportive to us and who lives in Staithes. She invited us up to her house at the top of the hill, for a glass of wine. As I was given a tour of her house by her young daughter, I couldn't help wondering what Georgina would have made of this blossoming friendship. I think she would have found it weird. She had absolute respect for Donna but was also a bit in awe of her.

It made me smile to think of Georgina watching me nibbling cheese and crackers and glugging chardonnay with her teacher. If Georgina had never become ill, Donna would still be the teacher who looks slightly impatient with us on open evenings as we dither about our darling's musical career options. How things change. So quickly. I would not have believed how far away eighteen months could carry us.

We've been playing again with the idea of moving house, but a shift down the coast to Staithes is no more do-able than jetting off into the Tenerife sunset. Paul's heart wouldn't handle the steep banks here. In practice – long-term - would we enjoy the remoteness? I think I might – I crave stillness – but I would need to be within reach of other human beings in case I suddenly hankered after hustle and bustle.

My mind is not to be trusted – I change it willy-nilly. It's telling me I'm hungry for change. Starving, in fact, because if the future's not going to be the way I initially imagined it, any changes might as well be radical. Now is not a time for half-cocked compromise and making-do, my mind is informing me. My heart and my mind are ganging up on me, telling me to go for broke. Get a move on. Go for it. None of us knows how much longer we are for this world. But there is another part of me – my waters or my soul – that warns against the burning of bridges. Be sensible. Slow down. Don't let grief make you do crazy, irreversible, regrettable things.

For now, my plan is to carry on keeping busy. I plan to carry on getting away from things on a temporary, manageable basis. It's all about distracting myself sufficiently to be able to keep on living. I promised my daughter I'd try to. Then, I promised her that I would actually do it. Tomorrow, we go home.

Tuesday, 3rd March 2015.

Today, I was reminded how important it is for me to write. Unstructured, free writing. I have started a therapeutic writing course being held in a converted school in the next town. The exercises we did in the first session caused me to reflect on the different ways in which various writing activities all contribute to my maintaining (give or take a bit) my equilibrium.

In this journal, I have mainly focused on Georgina, because I started this particular series of notebooks when Georgina was diagnosed. Even so, the entries have not all been directly 'about' Georgina. Sometimes, they have been about me and my attempts to sort myself out and lend myself some sort of shape again. Sometimes, I have set out to record and bear witness to this situation into which we have been catapulted. Sometimes, I write the first (and second and third) thing that comes into my head, even though I've not got anything particular to say, because I haven't known how to help myself. But I have known that I needed help.

I have also been writing my new novel (working title *All Hushed* – strictly subject to change). I have been pouring my deepest, darkest self into it. It is fiction, but it comes from a truthful place. I am organising my scribbled notes about grief by ascribing my conflicted feelings to characters who are – and yet most certainly are not – like me. I'm feeling my way towards my central message. I have several alternative endings to hand, but none of them have yet convinced me. *All Hushed* is coming out urgently and easily, compared to my first novel, *Blues*. I need to re-edit *Blues* and send it out to more potential agents, or years of effort on it will have been for nothing. But I'm not the same person who wrote that first book. I'm not even the same person who last trawled through it and chopped at it with a red pen. Maybe I'll give it a new name. Or I could leave it alone – a testament to how I was and how things were when I started writing it, three years ago. I still see flashes of myself in it. I still want to defend it. Both of my novels-in-progress about children being taken. Both are very real, and madly made-up, in their own ways.

My head often threatens to explode, so that I have to switch topics. At the therapeutic writing sessions, it's relaxing because I don't have to think about plot lines or imagery or viewpoint.

There is no set narrative arc and my life is not shaping itself into acts of equal length. I'm producing some okay stuff. I wonder why we demand such tight forms of our writing. Perhaps I'm cloaking laziness in the guise of a considered literary approach. Perhaps I'm choosing to be lax on structure because I'm just too tired to tighten things up.

I am so tired, I can't begin to tell you. But if I am so very tired, why do I stay up so very, ridiculously late? When the children were at home, I used to think I stayed up late because that was the only time that I could get the downstairs of the house to myself. Nowadays, that aloneness is no longer a rarity – I can pretty much orchestrate isolation at will. Maybe, the key to the attraction of the post-midnight hours is more the lack of interruptions. Long may people continue to think it impolite to knock or telephone after ten o'clock at night. It is late, now, but Paul has just come home from the Boro match, beside himself because "we" have won. "We" are top of the league. Yippee. I wish I didn't feel and sound so bitter. And I am truly glad that he is glad.

Sunday, 15th March 2015.

Helen Anderson posted:
A very emotional Mother's Day here. Lovely card and present from Joe Anderson. Looking forward to reacquainting myself with Thunderbird - my fave drink from my Birmingham Uni days. Lots of kind messages about Georgina from good friends. Yummy tea with my very own mum. Then

came home to find this beautiful bouquet and a thoughtful card from Georgina's girls. I am now a complete blubbering wreck, but thank you to everyone who's made me feel especially cared for today xxx

Monday, 30th March 2015.

Helen Anderson posted:
Thanks, Meg and Rob for a wonderful weekend in beautiful Shropshire. Lots of love to you all xxxxx

Monday, 6th April 2015.

Easter is so difficult, although it's our second without our daughter. I wasn't aware that Easter was a big event in our family calendar, but I miss not hiding chocolate eggs behind the curtains and announcing that the Easter Bunny has been. Paul and I went out for coffee and there were family groups all around us, in the café and everywhere. Logic tells me that there were lonely people, too, but the families stood out. I have to be careful not to stare at mothers with little children. I want to say "Imagine how you'd feel if you lost him/her. Hold him/her tight. Don't let go. Don't wish your life away. Don't sweat the small stuff."

When people don't look after their kids properly, but they still get to keep them, it strikes me as so unfair. I fed Georgina the right foods, and I smothered her in sun cream. I don't smoke and I didn't drink when I was pregnant, but still it happened. I took an interest in her schoolwork and ferried her to and from extra-curricular activities. No matter.

I got depressed. Sometimes, I couldn't pick myself up and I wasn't there. Or I was there in body, but not entirely in spirit. I am truly sorry for that. Every day, now, I beat myself up for wasting that time I could have had with Georgina. But, at the time, it didn't feel like a choice. I was just trying to stay alive – not to give in to the black desperation for which there was no obvious trigger. I was distracted by self-hatred and nameless terror. Later, I think that Georgina understood. When she herself felt down, she asked if that was how it had been for me and she tried to imagine coping with looking after children, while wanting to destroy yourself. We cuddled and I told her that she wouldn't grow up like me, because she'd stood up to her demons, early on. When Georgina was dying, she said "None of that matters now." What a gift it was that she gave me then. My daughter was a gift.

I am waiting for relatives to come round for Easter tea and they are late. I remember that none of that matters. I no longer sweat the small stuff, even if the garlic potatoes are burnt beyond a crisp. I want this house to be filled. It is so empty, with just the two of us. Four bedrooms for two of us. We could move house, but even a tiny cottage would have howling, aching voids. This house has been our family home, but our family has changed. I have been worrying a lot about Paul dying. This isn't so outlandish, given his health, and all my worst fears seem so possible, nowadays. Likely, even. Imminent, in fact. I don't know whether I could go on. I'm barely standing, even with Paul to lean on. One worry at a time. One step, then another. Piece by piece.

Saturday, 18th April 2015.

Shopping on a Saturday afternoon without my daughter. It doesn't feel right. I have nobody to consult about lipstick shades and candle scents. I try to imagine what Georgina would have to say about the clothes I'm considering buying but she's frozen in time. Fashions have changed, already.

Not having anyone to shop with is hardly the saddest aspect of this whole situation. It's a shallow complaint, coming from a deep, aching place. It hides an outrage, aggravated by the purchases which were supposed to so soothe: candle, plain trousers, skin cream, hairbrush. Half-hearted, impersonal buys.

In Café Nero, a five year old boy with Downs rests his head on my shoulder, curious to see what I'm scribbling. His mum calls him "cheeky" but there's no real chastisement in her voice. I'm glad. This is a mother who appreciates what she has.

Thursday, 23rd April 2015.

My mum has had a spooky experience. She didn't say "spooky", though. She said "strange", I think.

She had decided to move over to my late dad's side of the bed (eight years into widowhood), because she had a crick in her neck. In the middle of the night – she doesn't know exactly what time – she was woken by Georgina's song *Two Thirds of a Piece* playing on her mobile phone. One of Georgina's cousins downloaded it for her when it first came out, but if you asked Mum to play music on her phone, she wouldn't know where to start. She sometimes carries the phone with her if she's predicting an emergency or a communication, but apart from charging it every other night, she has minimal interaction with it. She doesn't know what time it was, but it was dark when Georgina's voice filled the room.

Mum was confused. She has no explanation for it. In the morning, she worked out how to play Georgina's song and she sat for a while to "have a think". My logical, stoical mother had tears in her eyes when she told me this stuff. I said that there must be some reasonable explanation – I can't bear to think that Georgina is aware of our every move but that we are unable to touch each other – but we couldn't come up with one, no matter how we tried. My mum proceeded to tell me about three times when (she thinks) my dad has tried to send her messages. She told me about the 'sympathy' – or perhaps 'telepathy'- she experienced with my dad as he lay in a coma and died. It all upset her, and yet it was a comfort. Did she feel foolish, telling me all this, when she has always been such a no-nonsense person? She says it has really made her think.

I called Paul, because I knew that it would please him to think of Georgina still being up there – still being mischievous. He chuckled and chuckled at her 'naughtiness' – typical Georgina. I, on the other hand, tried to apply logic and psychology to the whole story and to reason that a glitch had sent a blip to the phone in the dead of night and that my mum so wanted Georgina's energy to still be out there that she recounted it as fact. I would actually quite like it to be fact, so I nod and say "Maybe so" and "Who knows?"

I don't know – I wish I had absolute certainty that she is still out there, somewhere. It is mind-blowing to think that she might be trying to get a message to us. How I wish for that to be so. Georgina's friend has been asking around if anyone knows of a good spiritualist. A part of me would like to visit a medium and allow myself to be persuaded that it's not bunkum. I would love to be able to tell everyone what a sceptic I had been but that I – even I – had been persuaded by the intricacy and accuracy of my child's message to me. And if it happened that I thought it was bunkum, I could say that it had all been in the interests of research for my next book – a purely academic and investigative venture.

I, who have no faith or belief in anything but human beings and the here and now, would so like to be converted – to be convinced of something else – even though it pains me to be proven wrong to the extent that I can hardly even write the word "wrong"! To hear my darling girl, I would gladly be proven wrong, a hundred million times over.

Yesterday, I was at a workshop with the Finnish poet Claus Ankersen, and he made the case for all the energy that we put into our computers having to go somewhere else. There was much nodding and agreement. We were a room full of writers and poets, rather than scientists, but it didn't seem so far-fetched that one form of energy must turn into another. I am not exactly a trusting romantic, but I would risk ridicule amongst the staunchest of humanists/pragmatist/sceptics, gladly, for it to be true that she lives on.

In other news, I have a strong urge to tell people around me to f**** off. I hope that I won't shame myself and let a profanity slip out. I sometimes feel angry that I am required to rescue others but that no-one's rescuing me, except professionals who're paid to do so. I know that some friends and family are helping me, but I still feel so alone. And I want to rescue others because it helps me to make myself useful. I make no sense. I contradict myself. It's just that it would be a relief if someone saw through this 'coping' mask and contained my anxieties and grief for me.

I am floating above myself - watching this busy, capable me whirring in circles like a wind-up Santa. As I go about my business, I am silently saying "This is not really me". I talk to myself a lot, lately. All the time, this not really me. And yet, I keep on whirring and doing. I almost believe myself.

Last night, I had my dream where I'm phoning 999, but my fingers won't move and the numbers switch around on the keys.

Sunday, 26th April 2015.

Helen Anderson posted:
A busy-in-a-good-way weekend, going out Friday evening with pals. Then Saturday lunch to celebrate my lovely father-in-law's belated

birthday, now that he seems to be on the mend. Then, reading at the launch of Dark Matter 4 in Middlesbrough - with my son, Joe, in the audience at his very first poetry night. Today, a walk on the beach with Paul, Joe and Champ and a quick nip into the doggy-friendly part of The Ship. Just back from Darlington station, dropping Joe off, and trying to put aside Mummy-sadness to get on with my admin and hopefully some writing!

Wednesday, 29th April 2015.

I have broken my sunglasses, so I sneaked into Georgina's bedroom, to 'borrow' hers, knowing she'll never demand them back. I lingered in her room, talking to her. I caught sight of her tiny pyjamas. Pink rosebuds on cream linen. I picked up the jersey shorts that one of the nurses said weren't decent enough to be worn in the teenagers' lounge. I remember the way that the nurse covered Georgina's goosey legs with a holey, washed-out blanket, in front of her friends. Not a kind way.

I am going to London, again. I always want to write about Georgina, when I am on the train to London. It's a journey she loved. To Georgina, London was a strange, exotic place. A place where she could be herself. The place of her future. I wear her silver fingerprint around my neck.

Thursday, 30th April 2015.

On a hard wooden bench on a station platform in South East London. Thinking how much Georgina would have wanted to go shopping in Oxford Street or at Westfield Stratford. I have nobody to go shopping with, now.

Thinking what a shallow thing to think, after all Georgina went through. Like the Hickman line and all the pantomime of getting it in and out. I remember the shock of the Perspex tube, poking out of her collar-bone, when she came back from theatre. Her soft, biscuit-coloured skin was punctured first on the right side and – when that line grew a suspicious culture – on the left. I try to remember the procedure for cleaning and changing the line. We had to know it, or she wasn't allowed home. I can't recall all the steps.

Hopefully, I won't need that knowledge again. I try to think of something happier, but I'm torturing myself, now, with self-testing as to the mechanics of her feeding pump. I remember drawing bile from her swollen stomach, via her nose. How Paul eased that tube from her face, as soon as she died, because she'd asked him to. She hated that thing, stuck to her cheek, and scraping her voice-box.

I am meeting my son in the City for lunch in thirty minutes and I am on the verge of tears. I need to pull myself together and be there for him, so I put myself on the train to City Thameslink and I write this. My thoughts have to slow to the rate at which my fingers will transcribe them. The words ease away the miserable, hollow adrenaline.

<u>Sunday, 3rd May 2015.</u>

On the way home. For the rest of my time in London, I didn't write. My sister jokes that her house is a lethargy-pit at the moment and I did spend an inordinate amount of my time there snoozing. It was nice to snuggle down on the sofa with my sister, hiding under a woolly blanket.

I met Joe for lunch, as planned, and he was worryingly quiet. Afterwards, I navigated a still-being-built designer shopping centre and I didn't buy a thing, apart from Nurofen in Boots. I sat next to St. Paul's in dappled shade and marvelled at how far I've come – being out and about in London, all by myself. My sister and I both cried, in the evening.

I went for a run – okay, more of a fast walk – in Peckham Rye Park and my sister and her best friend and I recovered in the park café and we listed all the books we could think of which aren't cheerful and aren't packed with likeable characters. I went for a meal with my sister and my niece – a Girl's Night Out – and I missed my daughter. I went for a curry with all of my sister's family and we ordered too much. When we got home, we went back under the blanket, and my sister taught me how to crochet. Not the whole art. Just making a chain. Last time she tried to teach me, it was only a year since I'd fallen and broken my hand, and I couldn't hold the tension in the yarn. My hand mustn't be so broken, now.

My sister and my niece brought me all the way to King's Cross, although I've previously proven myself to be capable of negotiating the change at Elephant and Castle. They wanted to.

My niece cuddled into me on the Tube, because the announcer was way too loud. He really was. I missed my daughter. I miss and worry about my son.

Sunday, 3rd May 2015.

Helen Anderson posted:
I thought 'The C-Word', starring Sheridan Smith, was well written and acted. But it made me so sad that Georgina didn't even get a 'treatment break' in which to do a few enjoyable things, because her disease progressed so super-fast. This probably makes me a very bad person, being ever-so-slightly jealous of poor/wonderful Lisa Lynch.
— feeling confused.

Wednesday, 6th May 2015.

Out and about in my hometown. I keep thinking that people are talking about me. I find that some people hold my gaze for a fraction too long and their eyes switch to pity-mode. It might well be my imagination.

I go to the dentist. I go to the manicurist. I have my various bits attended to. I wish they had proper access to my inside: that I could get my mood professionally cleaned and polished. In the coffee shop, I think the assistant may have given me too much change. She is convinced that I gave her £10, whereas I thought it was £5. I am worried that she has long-changed me. I leave my telephone number, in case she gets in trouble when they reckon up. I leave my name, and I think that I spy that too-long flash of recognition.

It might be my imagination. She never calls, so I suppose she must have been right, all along.

Friday, 8th May 2015.

In Newcastle for the Teenage Cancer Trust's Fifth Birthday Ball. It's the first time I've been back in this city since we took Georgina home to die. As we crossed the Tyne in the ambulance that day, I said that I'd had enough of Newcastle, and Georgina told me off.

"Don't say that. I've always loved Newcastle."

For Georgina, as it had been for me, it had been a place for concerts and theatre and Christmas shopping trips, way before the hospital dominated the landscape. It is a place of good memories, as well as horrendous ones, and I don't want to avoid it forever.

Our hotel room has a view of the stadium at St James' Park. There is a similar view of the other side of the structure from the Teenage Cancer Trust penthouse lounge at the hospital. Those steel struts are all too familiar. I feel as if Georgina must be waiting for me, downstairs, in a side room. I'd give anything to have her back, even at that stage. Which is selfish of me, as she felt very sick.

Two years ago, my daughter was a schoolgirl and a busker and we could not have guessed what would come. Eighteen months ago, I could still hold her slender hands and nuzzle her fuzzy, baldy head. I miss those things. But it's not about what I miss – it's about the things that she deserved and will never have.

Tonight, we will dress up and go out and celebrate the fun and spirit that she brought into our lives. I will put on the glitz and I will be glam. I will have a ball, for my lost girl.

<u>Saturday, 9th May 2015.</u>

It was both difficult and lovely to see members of staff who worked with Georgina at the hospital. We saw the amazingly energetic teenage activities co-ordinator, Cara, and a down-to-earth social worker, Maureen, and a kind student nurse who came over to introduce herself and is now fully qualified. They all remember Georgina, even though she was only in treatment for three months or so. The nurse wanted us to know that the members of staff haven't forgotten her. Maureen pronounced us a "canny" family and declared that Georgina was especially beautiful. They all think about her and about us a lot and they think we're very brave. I didn't feel very brave, last night.

We met a bereaved parent who was helping out at the event, who Paul knows from an internet support group. She lost her son in 2011 and she still leaves his trainers out in the hall, alongside the rest of the family's shoes. His brother still wears bright, odd socks, because that was the lost boy's trademark, when he was in hospital.

Back at the hotel, I had a good cry. Two minutes, at least. It was hard, but I feel that I achieved something, just by coming back.

This morning, at breakfast, I talked to a charity worker whose daughter had kidney and lung cancer when she was four years old. The child is now fourteen. This lady feels guilty that her child survived. Then, she feels guilty about feeling guilty about her own child living.

Thursday, 14th May 2015.

People said that they wouldn't forget Georgina, but how can I tell? They are getting on with their exams and their prom dresses. They are continuing with their petty squabbles. Do I look like I'm forgetting, too, as I meet my friend for coffee and work out the wording for a writing mentoring application?

I have not forgotten. The aim of all this is distraction. Getting through. Just one more day; hour; minute. Perhaps other people, too, frenzy themselves so as to forget.

Monday, 18th May 2015.

Buoyed up by the huge reaction to the piece I wrote about Georgina's illness and death. *What A Girl Wants* was published online in the University of Illinois' *Compass Literary Magazine*. My link to the article has been shared many times over and people have messaged me saying that it has made them cry. This is the stuff that I feel I really need to write, but I'm anxious not to strike an over-sentimental or sensationalist tone, I want to honour Georgina's memory – to tell it as I see it and how I remember it. And if it helps others to understand, or to not feel so alone, then so much the better. The main thing for me is for Georgina to be remembered and for our story to be heard.

I've been training for the Race for Life 5k run. 5km isn't far for some people, but it's a big deal for a fatty like me. I have started receiving sponsorship, so it's becoming real. It's not like I'm jumping from a plane for charity, but I've had to force myself out there and stick at the training. It's a small thing and it's a big thing. My left knee is aching and swollen, but I haven't crumbled yet.

Today, I went to Harlow Carr Gardens near Harrogate, with my friend, Karen. Karen is a neighbour, a writer and a young widow. Our circumstances have thrown us together. We admired the rhododendrons and the Himalayan poppies. I bought delicate blue flox, to pretty up our patch at home. There's something comforting about seeing nature blooming, in a managed way.

We had lunch and we shared our stories of loss. We have so much and so little in common. It felt good to be able to raise a glass of wine to my daughter and to Karen's husband, in the middle of the day. We ate cake and we agreed that there's no romance in cancer. There's definitely no glamour. It isn't pretty, how the body deteriorates. But Georgina was still beautiful.

I saw Georgina today, in the fragile veins on a lilac petal bearing the heaviness of dew. The gnarled red trunks of pink rhododendrons reminded me of my trip to the Lost Gardens of Heligan with my mum, just before Georgina fell ill. She must already have been ailing, but we didn't know it. So many petals have fallen, in these two years. So much is different but the flowers are blooming yet again and they are still beautiful enough to stop me in my tracks.

I am still alive. If I look too far ahead, it all seems impossible. If I focus on the moment, it seems too short – too tiny – to matter. I need to set my sights on the middle-distance, but it's hard to keep your concentration when you know that it can be grabbed from you, just like that.

I remind myself time after time that I must value this life, because it's a gift that Georgina wasn't allowed to keep. It sounds like a motivational poster or a social media meme, put like that. But I don't want to be ungrateful for this thing that Georgina would have given anything for. If she thought it was worth fighting for – and she DID fight – then I'll trust her judgement. My daughter was a wise one. I will fight, too, even if I can't quite put my finger on the reason why. I hope that I will be able to continue to fight. I plan to. I hope that God or Fate or Whatever doesn't see that as a direct challenge.

Friday, 29th May 2015.

I envy people who still have children to worry themselves sick about. I try not to make other parents feel awkward when they moan about teenage strops and mess-making.

I've spent a few days with my brother and his family. It was lovely but being around my brother's teenage children made me ache. I took my niece shopping but it didn't help the ache. Nothing does. I can't replace my own girl. Now, my sister and her children are up north, visiting, for half-term.

People talk an awful lot about their kids, then they realise and they are embarrassed. So they ask "Does Joe do this or that?" They seem glad that Paul and I still have Joe to talk about, even though Georgina is gone, so that they needn't feel so bad about still having children of their own. How awful it must be to have lost an only child. This loss of our daughter is terrible enough, but what a life-shock, suddenly not being the parent of anyone who is alive, any more.

We are in a strange situation, because our surviving child isn't around, geographically-speaking. He is forging ahead with his own life, which happens to be away from here, as we have urged him to do. Also, he is grown-up because there was a five and a half year age-gap between him and his little sister. So, I don't know quite where we fit in. Suddenly, we are empty-nesters.

I ache to be around my son. He came to see us at my brother's house and it hurt to be a mother again – to have to say goodbye to him. I don't want to hold him back in his life, but I want to clutch him to me. He seems extra-precious, but he doesn't appreciate being told that. I tell him anyway. There's no room for leaving things unsaid.

Sometimes, I ache so badly for Georgina that I wonder how many more days I am expected to survive like this. How have I survived eighteen months without her? It feels like treachery. Yet it would be a betrayal of her to throw the towel in, now, after all this wading through desperate times. I can't believe this has happened to us. I pinch myself and it really hurts – everywhere – and I know I'm wide awake.

Friday, 5th June 2015.

Coffee in Middlesbrough. I am shopping. I am on my own. It's a depressing experience, but so is staying in. Having no decent clothes is also depressing.

Last night, Paul said a nice thing to me – that he so loves the person I've become in recent years. What I heard was that he mustn't have loved me as I was before. I think I may be depressed, but when I have been properly depressed in the past, I couldn't leave the house for months. At the moment, they keep hitting me – dark flashes of doom cutting through my best shiny-happy performances. I have taken to swearing a lot in the car, with Christina Aguilera drowning out my profanities with "You are beautiful".

There's a strange numbness about me. I have mixed feelings about having no feelings. When you need a tooth extracted, nobody would try to persuade you that you'd be better off facing the pliers without an anaesthetic. But the wisdom seems to be that I need to feel this emotional pain, without the benefit of lidocaine. Some say that healing is to be found in suffering. Numb me up, any time. I can take a sharp scratch. Then, nothing.

Thursday, 11th June 2015.

Yesterday, Georgina's year-group left school and it's hard to avoid being bombarded by Facebook pictures of them with scribbled-on shirts and leavers' books. They are climbing one another's shoulders and posing with teachers and congratulating each other on making it through school. My daughter did not make it through school: she missed two whole years, bar the day or two of Year 10 that she managed to attend, complete with feeding-tube and real-hair wig.

I am so envious, I can't look at myself. I am so jealous, I can't look at Facebook. I know that Georgina's friends' lives have to go on, but it is so hard. It is too hard. Have they forgotten her and us, so soon? I don't think so, really. I know that it's just about getting on and getting through, for all of us. A girl in Georgina's year has been very ill, but her mum told Paul that when they think things are bad, they look at us and remember that things could be worse. It's hard to be such a consolation.

I feel as if someone's trampling on my chest, to the extent that I'm struggling to write; to exercise; to think straight. I want to make a tent out of blankets and to put my fingers in my ears. I am overloaded – in overdrive – but when I look at my diary objectively, I haven't really got too many obligations. My brain is firing off into a thousand directions: firing blanks into blackest space.

I want to shout extremely bad swear-words. I don't shout them, but I mumble to myself in Tesco's. It's the only way I can get around a supermarket, by giving myself mini pep-talks. I have tinnitus – thankfully, not voices, but whizzing rockets and screeching mosquitos. I have a headache. This is Too-Much-Information, but I even have constipation. I am off-kilter. Off-key. Discordant.

I want my mum. When my mum comes round, she drives me into a state of even greater nervousness. No-one can comfort me. Paul has been trying, by cooking tea and offering paracetamol and glasses of water. We are glad to have each other (This has not always been the case, through our thirty-year relationship).

Next week, I am going with my mum on holiday to Norway. I want to get away, but I don't want to stray too far from home. I just don't know where I want to be, because I don't know IF I want to be. I will feel guilty if I enjoy myself, and I will feel guilty if I waste this chance to see more of this world – a chance Georgina wasn't given. Each new day is taking me further away from my daughter. Her dressing-gown still smells of her, if I close my eyes tight, and inhale and hold my breath until I nearly faint.

Last week we met more bereaved parents at a meeting organised by the hospital. Most of them had lost a child even more recently than we have and I felt as though I had to act like a wiser, older parent to these relative newbies to this terrible grief. Many of them were crying, and I was even jealous of their tears, because my tears have gone AWOL again: maybe they have migrated to my chest and are building up there, like a tumour that's about to burst its walls. Metastatic misery.

We sat on chairs set out in a circle, and we mothers held our children's silvered fingerprints between the fleshy pads of our thumbs and forefingers. Those pendants around our necks are like a membership badge of a club nobody wants to join. They hang like medals. Another aching mother told me that she kisses the mark taken from the imprint of her dead son's hand. Me, too.

"Me, too." The mumble went around the circle. It was an exquisite, agonising kind of belonging.

<u>Saturday, 13th June 2015.</u>

I went to my dad's grave, because I normally go on Father's Day. However, next week, on Father's Day, I will be on a fjord cruise with my mum. This is okay, because I promised my dad I'd look after my mum, as we stood at the hole into which his coffin was lowered. I haven't always done an excellent job of keeping that promise, but I think my dad would be glad that we are off on our jollies together. I had a little chat with Dad about it, and I was not struck down with lightning, so I think that it must be okay for us to go on the Flam railway and the Foss Falls (something like that), from my dad's point of view.

We were in mid-conversation when I heard the cemetery gates clink. I thought it would be kids, so I shut up. It was a young woman who had several bunches of flowers tucked under her arms. I wondered how many graves she was visiting – what multiple misfortunes had befallen her family – but she headed to a single patch, at the end of my dad's row. I was careful not to stare, but I could see that she was kneeling down, rolling a necklace or a silver charm between her fingers. She piled those flowers on a single, unmarked plot. She knelt, letting the grass soak her jeans.

It had been raining overnight, so the brass vase for my dad's flowers was full of liquid slime. It took it to the cemetery tap. I hosed it down and filled it with fresh water. I placed it back in front of the shiny black slab that denotes the resting place for my dad's bones, and I slotted twelve stems of orange roses into the metal grid on the top. I had trimmed the stems to the optimum length, so that the wind wouldn't catch them. They looked strong. I explained to my father about my holiday plans. I told him about Georgina, though surely he must know, by now, by heavenly means or if he actually listens to me on these visits.

The woman at the end was still unwrapping each bunch; laying each flower on the designated area of freshly turned earth, one by one. Back at my car, I drove to the end of the lane to a suitable point for my six-point turn. When I doubled back, she was still at it. I could see her lips moving, as if she was singing, but I don't know how, because I was quite far away. Once, I saw a different woman prostrate on a different, anonymous plot and I thought that it couldn't be normal, to lie spread-eagled like that over interred remains. She clawed at the ground. She was silent. I told my friend about it, and she agreed it wasn't normal. I told my doctor about it, and he agreed it wasn't normal. Pathological grief, possibly.

My grief for my dad felt suitably contained and appropriately expressed in those twelve, thorn-free stems, but as I bumbled home, singing along to Smooth Radio classics, I worried that my comparative composure might be disrespectful. Then, I remembered how displays of emotion used to make him squirm, even while he flushed with pleasure; how he preferred to deal with difficulties by means of a joke. I hummed along, smiling inside.

It is nearly nine years since my dad died, and I miss him but accept that he has gone. If Georgina had a grave, I fear that the rawness of my grief would have me floundering atop a heap of floral tributes or scrabbling at the ground like these bereaved women, in an undignified, decidedly non-decorous fashion. I wish she had a grave. It is probably a good job that she does not.

Friday, 19th June 2015.

Norwegian fjordland cruise. I am never at home. We are at sea, the announcement over the loudspeaker confirms. The ship is throbbing and swaying and keeping our air properly conditioned. I sit in on of the many lounges, at sea, listening to the hiss of a machine supplying a vessel at full capacity with hot beverages. I am surrounded by older people, discussing their previous cruises. These war-time babies have had their fair share of austerity and they are out to enjoy life.

My mum worries that the scene is not lively enough for me, but I reassure her. We explore the ship, with its handrails and its foreboding *Watch Your Step* signs. My mum is impressed at how often I remember to use the hand-gel which is stationed at every corner, to prevent the spread of the dreaded Norovirus. When you've got a child with cancer, I tell her, you get good at remembering to sanitise. When you have *had* a child with cancer, I mean. We sit on the deck, gazing at the grey-blue North Sea. There is a lot of it. I tilt my face towards the white Nordic sun and let the waves rock me.

Twice, today, I have mentioned Georgina, because I need to hear her name and nobody on this ship will say it. My mother is managing not to flinch, and even leaves a respectable interval before changing the subject. She is not one to dwell on things, especially on holiday. Tonight, we will meet the Captain and the heads of various nautical departments. They will receive us in formal attire at 7.15 p.m. I like being a gift about to be given.

Muzak is piped over the speakers. *Forever Young.* Oh, the irony. Some of these pensioners look like they want to live forever, and they might. I don't want to. Not forever. Not now. Just for as long as I can bear. I don't tell Mum this.

<u>Sunday, 21st June 2015.</u>

In the ship's gym. I have promised myself half an hour on the cross-trainer. I may be in the middle of a fjord, but there is still a race to train for. I run on the spot, while the ship is moored to a quay in an inlet. The water outside is green and undisturbed. I contemplate the difference between a fjord and a lagoon. I can't Google it because I haven't paid for Wi-Fi because the signal is intermittent. This time next week, the Race for Life will be over. One way or another, I will be done. Will I be done, or will I still have a way to go? I keep striding out on this eternal conveyor belt.

Today, we went on an excursion and saw turf-roofed cabins and rainbow waterfalls. We heard about juniper berries and Grieg's Opus 66 and the lemmings which disappear every four years. We heard about rock-slides and shape-shifting trolls turning into mountain-mermaid-thingies with cow-tails and four fingers. I think that's what they said. Definitely, the trolls are allergic to sunlight - it makes them explode into avalanches. We saw pine trees and drank coffee at a half-melted ski-lodge.

Through the window, I watch yellow kayaks being paddled to shore by figures in orange jackets. The flags on the quayside hang still on their masts. I debate which white and red wooden house on the hillside will become mine, when I am finally living my true, dream life. It is a tantalising fantasy. Not quite impossible, surely, if I put my mind to it, and with a bit of luck. It is rush-hour on the only road stitched around the neck of the water. There are five silver flashes, like trout-skin. I count them. The ship rocks and lulls. I fear that I'll fall asleep on this treadmill, on this longest of days. The sunlight makes patterns dance on the walls. Both my children were entranced by their Lullaby Light Show toy, which projected beams and shapes across their darkened nursery ceiling. How do they ever put a child down to sleep, here, in this land of the forever-bright sun?

I move to the deck, to cool down before returning to my cabin. Laughter spurts up from below. I wonder if they have ever known this pain, and how they learned to live on until their hair was white like the snow in the crevices of the

252

craggy mountains. The ice is melting – theatrically falling into spring. It is the talk of the ship, how late the Norwegian Spring is, this year. Some say that they have switched straight to mid-summer. The silver birch trees frantically sprout their greenery as though they are in a fast-motion film. The catkins on the willows take their time: they are not yet ripe.

A speed boat scours the smooth surface, veering a little too close for comfort. The season is definitely changing. The ship sets sail, and its wake zigzags behind us like a cardiac trace.

Monday, 22nd June 2015.

We look down on the city of Bergen from the carpeted sun-deck. My Tesco sun cream warms in its yellow bottle, next to my lounger. Don't think it's always this hot here, they warn us - this place has a reputation for rain. They've made a little joke of it, specialising in umbrella shops. Today, the streets were sizzling as we saw for miles at the top of the hill and strolled through the markets underneath it. Conversation at the dinner tables has centred on the sky-high cost of living; the average monthly salary; when the oil fields are due to run out. There is a lot of land, per Norwegian person. So much sea, stretching before us. Tomorrow, we will head back to Britain. We will dock in a different port and disperse.

My mum is in a grumbly mood. Dissatisfaction hovers over us like a gull over a herring stall. I tell her not to be so down on herself. I regret all the years when I, too, was so discontented with my lot and with me. I regret the regret and that I no longer have a daughter to advise to be kind to herself. All those lessons I have finally learnt about the pointlessness of self-loathing, and no-one to receive my knowledge. Rather, not quite "no-one" – I have a son who could benefit from cutting himself a little slack. I make a note to remind him.

The person on the adjacent sun bed has beautiful white feet, with pink, clipped nails. An iridescent sheen hints at a future bunion. A single vein protrudes – a pale grey worm cast - on the arch from ankle to middle toe. The tendons flex, registering the fjord breeze on her hairless extremities. The sun goes behind a cloud. We are about to depart. The feet shuffle into Fit-Flops and the owner rises from a horizontal position to reveal the rest of her. This squat, thin-haired old lady does not quite belong to her lower limbs.

I watch the city grow smaller. When architects dream of copper spires, do they envisage them as orange beacons, or are they resigned to their ageing and greening? I choose a blue, mustard and white wooden house by the water's edge - my new fantasy retreat.

We have been delayed by thirty minutes by Julie and Robert from Cabin 214. They have failed to board. Arrival time will not be affected. In another two hours, we will be disembarking the pilot and leaving the shelter of the fjords for the open sea. Perhaps Julie and Robert have decided to stay – chosen the colour of their hut, along with a forever-location on the shoreline. It isn't always sunny here. In fact, as they keep reminding us, it's most unusual. For 240 days each year – 266 days, according to one leaflet – it rains. I hope that the missing couple have remembered that. I hope they haven't made any rash decisions and burned their (mainly suspension) bridges.

Tuesday, 23rd June 2015.

At sea. I am writing for an hour, to let my afternoon tea go down before I toddle off to the gym again to make room for my evening meal. In five days' time, it is the big run, and I am not race-fit. I console myself with the promise of a super-renewed final effort, jogging over my home ground.

I try to find a quiet spot where I might gather my thoughts, but the ship is full. Today, we are all aboard and all indoors. The people nearest me consider the dark Meccano angles of the oil rigs balancing in the swollen sea. They think that they must be lighthouses, and they cannot imagine why they have been put there. Although this is my quiet spot, I am not good at not paying attention to other people's conversations. I am a born eavesdropper. There are worse traits for a writer to possess.

I start to think about the number of e-mails that will be waiting for me, once I'm reconnected to land. Dread (so much to do) and hope (maybe I'll have been discovered in my absence). The day after tomorrow would have been Georgina's prom. I need to go away again as soon as I get back. Or, at least, stay off the internet until Facebook is clear of the excited anticipation and the photos of the event and the post-event events. This weekend, Joe is coming home. I love that he wants to spend time with his parents, but it worries me, too, because it means that he is not feeling settled. We have all been rather rocky, recently. Hence our new, vintage campervan. And the hut-on-the-hill fantasies.

The people at the next table didn't think much of the Captain's Q and A session, what with the Captain being Greek and his English being so stilted. It all fell a bit flat. Conversation turns again to the Nordic economy. We can't get over the price of woolly hats and fish and chips. It's not a cheap holiday, but the fjords are stunning. And we have been so lucky with the weather. Haven't we? This is the quietest spot I can wangle.

They are setting the table for the evening buffet that they put on for those who prefer to dine casually. They are putting blue table cloths on the bistro tables, to shift the ambience from day to night. The man on the table next to me didn't bring a formal suit. It was a deliberate decision, but now he wonders if he's missed out. He wouldn't have minded a photo with that Captain.

Conversation turns to holidays, past, present and future. Probably Turkey, in October. They'll go All Inclusive, although he doesn't like to just lounge about all day. He was there in May and it was red hot. The situation in Syria doesn't affect Turkish holidays; it hasn't made them any cheaper. The lady with him states that Portugal is a bit dull. They went up into the hills, one day, but apart from that there wasn't much to do even for a week. New Zealand, mind. Now, that's nice. I look for a quieter quiet spot.

Tuesday, 30th June 2015.

On Sunday, I ran the Race for Life. It's only 5km, but I've been preparing for that race for months. In truth, I mostly walked – but fast. And with little jogs to get ahead of slow groups, and at the end, when everyone was watching. I cried when the route took us through the Middlesbrough Football Club stadium, and alongside the pitch. The last time I was next to that pitch – on that very same pitch – I was pushing Georgina in her wheelchair. It was four days before she died. I kept a smile on my face, for her and for the crowd. This time, I cried. Nobody came to my rescue, so I jogged on.

I was running alone. I'm sure that if I'd asked friends to do the race with me, they would have done, but I kind of discouraged anybody from joining in, as I wanted to do this thing by myself and to train for it in my own way. It was like a contract between Georgina and me, and I didn't want anyone else involved in it. I felt good in my t-shirt with Georgina's picture in a star-shape on my front, and "Georgina's Mum" printed on each sleeve. Joe and Paul came with me to watch. It felt like a nice family thing to do – a way to pay our respects to the one missing from our four.

I have raised £1,300 for Cancer Research UK. It helped keep me going – the thought that such an amount of sponsorship warranted at least an attempt at a jog. My mum didn't come to watch. She muttered something about there being too much standing around. But afterwards she said that she wished she'd come, and she brought round some flowers and a card. She knows how hard I've tried to keep going, with the running and everything. It feels good that my mum is proud of me. I am keeping going with my keeping fit, because it would be against the spirit of my contract with Georgina, if I were to give up straight away. No marathons for me, though. Definitely not.

This last week would also have been Georgina's prom. It was hard, as expected, to be gracious about the photos of hair, nails, make-up and frocks which flooded my social media. I felt bad about feeling so jealous. I wanted Amber and the rest of Georgina's friends to enjoy themselves – their having a crap prom wouldn't bring Georgina back - but a horrible part of me wanted them to notice that someone was missing. Paul and I agreed with each other that our daughter would have been the prettiest girl there and that we're not even the tiniest bit biased. Some of the boys wore pink ties, and some of the girls had pink rose corsages. My girl was remembered – I need not have worried about that.

Nowadays, apparently, they have a 'Prom Breakfast' in school, the morning after the night before. We were invited in. We were asked to walk at the back of the parade of revellers who made it back into school, after an evening at a stately home and a night in the woods. The current students formed a guard of honour and applauded us all. It felt like a great big hug from the entire school. Georgina's absence was acknowledged so that she almost became a presence.

There was a balloon release in her memory, for her peer group, and it felt like a fitting ending – as if she is moving on with her friends as they leave school, rather than being stuck in Year 10 forever. The young people had asked for Georgina's name to go on the Leavers' sweatshirt, along with all her friends'. The teachers presented us with a pink hoody with her name printed amongst the others, and Paul draped it around his shoulders. These are good people – these young people and their teachers. Georgina's friend Abbie was asked to give a little speech and it was perfect. It struck me, how fast they've had to grow up, to cope with this adult-sized grief. The tone of the send-off was just right. It marked the end of an era – vastly different for Georgina and for us than it should have been – in a sad, beautiful way. It felt as right as it possibly ever could have done.

Paul has gone away for a few nights with Big Paul. Our internet has been down, so I have been working on my new novel and writing up these diaries into *Piece by Piece*. Going over these past few months – the process of typing my scribbled notes – is hard. Yet, it feels necessary. I am breaking it down into almost-manageable pieces. Chunks. I miss Paul, because he is the only one who I know really understands this awful misery-ache. He will be back soon, and he will probably get on my nerves. We may bicker, but we are partners, especially in this. He will be back soon.

It has occurred to me that I will need to decide, at some point, to stop telling this story of mine. Or at least I may need to stop telling it out loud to other people – I think that I will always write about losing and having Georgina, in one way or another. They say that the things that are most important to a writer find a way to shine through. But, at some point, I must choose an ending for *Piece by Piece*. It will not stop me from continuing to be Georgina's Mum.

Sunday, 5th July 2015.

Helen Anderson posted:
Single pink rose laid by Paul and myself at the cancer ward's memory day, yesterday. Surrounded by tributes to some of the other children from the North East who didn't make it through their battle. Mind blowing and sad to think how many people are affected. Xxxxxx

Tuesday, 7th July 2015.

South London. Mum and I are minding my sister's children, while my sister and her husband go on holiday to celebrate my sister's birthday. I encouraged them to go – I practically insisted on it. They need a break and they haven't had one together since my niece stayed over with us when she was two. She is almost fourteen, now. They definitely deserve a break.

I want to be a good aunty. I have always tried to be active in their lives – to be a presence, even though we live two hundred and fifty miles apart – but there is an urgency to the relationship, now. There is probably a selfishness to my enjoyment of the cuddles and the joking around, but my sister's children are very much their own people. My niece is quite unlike my own girl, in lots and lots of ways, so she would be a most unlikely stand-in for her, even if there was any question of even attempting to make her fill the Georgina-shaped void.

However, I need to be around youth and the hope that comes with it. I need to nurture, and that particular part of myself has been forced to focus all its energies on Joe, who is actually grown-up and has need of me in less obvious, less direct ways. My adult son would probably willingly regress and let me baby him, if he thought it would make me feel even slightly better. But that really would be selfish, on my part. I want him to feel safe and held, but not constricted.

I know that I need to let him continue to venture out into the world, however much I would like to bring him back home and keep him close to me, geographically and emotionally. In all practical senses, Joe is back to being an only child – as he was for the five and a half years before Georgina was born - yet that is not quite his status. He is not the only child to whom I am a mother.

I worry that other mothers will worry that I am trying to borrow their kids. When Amelia was going off to her prom, Caytie invited me over to see her dress and to wave her off. Amelia has been part of our lives for many years, but I almost didn't go, because I didn't want to make everybody feel awkward. In the end, I went, because it was less weird than not going. She looked beautiful. She gave me a hug and things got a bit emotional. Sometimes, I imagine – I am quite sure that it is my imagination – that people view me as a potential child-thief. I am wary of seeming too interested in other people's kids' lives, in case that interest is deemed unhealthy. Nobody has said such a thing to me, but bereaved mothers in the news and in the movies are unstable, unpredictable creatures. I have time on my hands and clear days in my diary and I am determined to be the best aunty and friend that I can be. But I know the limits. And the only children I want to catch are my own.

In cafés, sometimes, I catch myself watching young families and wanting to tell the mothers to cherish their children – that they are gone sooner than you think. What I would give to go back to that time when my two were small – that time which I found so difficult. When I thought it might be easier when they got older. I want to go back and enjoy them, instead of worrying and feeling swamped and depressed. I want to un-wish my wishing that they'd grow up faster.

Monday, 20th July 2015.

We have brought our new (1980s) campervan out on a trial run. We have pitched up and plugged in at a site thirty miles from our home, to test everything. To test whether we are the stuff campers are made of. Blobs of tepid, grey rain release the exotic, coconut fragrance of my suncreamed, chilled limbs.

Last night, our newly-acquired carbon-monoxide alarm went off at 5.30 a.m. It's very sensitive. It was an early-morning early-warning. It was shrill. Paul was convinced that we were about to die. Just now, I have checked the leaflet that came with it and we were only marginally over the 'safe' limit. But we both have headaches. I dismiss mine as a souvenir of disturbed sleep, but Paul takes his as proof of our brush with the Grim Reaper. We have unplugged the fridge and opened all the windows and the sunroof. Paul will look at the fridge vent properly, when we get home. We were so pleased that the thirty-year-old appliance actually cooled things down that we forgot to check its connection to the outside. Whoops. At least the wine and the Diet Cokes were nice and cold. We'd have died feeling refreshed.

Paul is going over our 'lucky' escape in a forensic way that makes me question whether he really would have found further misfortune so very terrible. He wonders who would have found us. He wonders if they'd have thought we'd agreed upon a suicide pact – taken the dog with us to see Georgina. He wonders if God saved us, or was trying to punish us and messed up. He wonders (out loud) if Georgina wants us to come to be with her. We think (together and out loud) how awful it would have been for our son to be the only one left. We promise to jam the windows open tonight. We will drink warm wine and make sandwiches with oily spread and lukewarm cheddar. Paul will get to the bottom of the fumes detected, once we are home.

Such a lucky escape we agree. Best not to dwell on it.

Monday, 3rd August 2015.

Camping in North Yorkshire. I am lying on a rug on the grass next to our campervan. Black harvest flies crawl over the page of my notebook, ignoring its printed lines. A warm wind rushes through the trees and the meadow grass.

At the bottom of the field is a block of sandstone, carved with "Where there are trees, there is always music." I like this. I think that it is true, even if the music is more like percussion than violin – a gentle, rhythmic brushing on the skin of a drum. I wonder who came up with the saying. I must Google it, when I get the chance, though I try to keep off my electronics when I'm communing with nature.

The stone is a memorial for a certain Joanna, whose dates make her nineteen. I wonder about her. I wonder if they would mind us using the same phrase on a memorial seat for Georgina. We have been meaning to organise a bench by the beach or in the woods. I must contact the Council, when we get back. At the top of the hill opposite the field is a stone seat – chiselled with initials and "1911 – 2005". Ninety-four seems a whole lot fairer.

The farmer guides a monster motorhome onto the grass in front of the dry stone wall. I will its wheels to keep on turning. I don't want the shiny white metal to spoil my view of the shadows shifting across this scarred, gorse-swathed valley. The pigs are being fed. I want to urge them to make a run for it, before they end up in one of the farm's famous sausages. I wonder what they make of the smell of charred flesh rising up from the camp barbecues.

My thoughts shift to the new crematorium near our town. In the local paper's photos, it looks bright and airy, with its soothing fountains and its contemporary gardens. I hope that they have a big waiting room. In all the services I've ever been to in other, older crematoriums, the queuing for the right funeral has not been a dignified affair. They usher the next lot in while they're still playing *What a Wonderful World* for the coffin that's just gone behind the curtain.

At Georgina's funeral, the crematorium bit was awful. The hearse had to queue to get onto the driveway. While they cleared the chapel of the previous party, we shivered outside, serenaded by a kilted piper who was nothing whatsoever to do with Georgina. It was almost funny. It was surreal. It compounded my feeling that the whole thing was a terrible mistake: that we really should not have been there, at all.

Monday, 10th August 2015.

I am up late. I am watching the music channels on TV, like the old days. I don't recognise the Hits of 2015: Summer has passed me by. I switch to *Relax and Unwind*, where I know the songs. I could write out all the lyrics from the past – I like to say them a line ahead of the singer – but there doesn't seem any point to learning contemporary pieces. I am lost. I have fallen too far behind, already. I used to stay up when the rest of the family had gone to bed, committing the newest words and melody to memory so that I could impress Georgina with my up-to-the-minute musical knowledge. The next morning, I'd drop a reference to a singer, oh-so-coolly-and-casually, into the conversation. I couldn't keep up.

One flick of the remote, and I am in my comfort zone. I feel almost cutting-edge, singing along with hip tune after hip tune. Until I realise it's 'Guess the Year'. And the year is 2005. In 2005, Georgina was seven years old. I like it there, in Classics territory. There, I can pretend that nothing's changed.

Sunday, 6th September 2015.

Feeling nervous about approaching people I've mentioned in my diaries for their approval. I am seeking their permission to write about them, as a courtesy, but I am desperate to tell my story as I have experienced it. I want to get it out there. My story's no good in my head or stuck in notebooks, however pretty my stationery collection might be. I wonder when I'll be strong enough to read Georgina's notebooks. I wonder what I'll find. I have no doubt that Georgina's version of events will be very different from mine, because she and I were very different people. Although her diary stopped on Day Three, there are stacks of books of lyrics and chords which I will brave. One day.

Georgina and I have both written for ourselves, all the time knowing that someone in the future might read our scribbles and reach into our minds and spirits even when we are no longer here. I like to think that Georgina would have wanted me to be bold with this project. Paul thinks so. Georgina's song-writing was a way of communicating of emotions that she found it hard to express in a more direct way.

When her people were tweeting the link to her YouTube video, they used the hashtag #cancercannotsilencehervoice. It's a fine sentiment, and she can still be heard via the many recordings that we are so lucky to have been left with. But I'm aware that I cannot speak for her. I have no right. Georgina didn't like me to speak for her, even when she was alive. She was a girl with her own views and her own ways of framing them.

In publishing these diaries, I will be speaking only for myself. This is the story of a mother plunged into mourning, out of the brightest, bluest nowhere. I write because it keeps me afloat, helping me to tread water and take gulps of air. One day, with a bit of luck and improved stamina, I might feel strong enough to strike out for the shore. I may have written this journal for selfish, therapeutic purposes, but I hope that it will show others who find themselves in similar, terrible circumstances that it is possible to keep on. Even when it seems out of the question.

I don't want to seem smug: I can well imagine that this statement (some would call it a platitude) may turn on me and bite a massive chunk out of my backside, at some point. But, for now, I am getting through by following the example of an unthinkably strong, unbelievably resourceful young woman who I am proud to claim as my daughter.

Georgina Louise Anderson, thank you for showing us how to survive, when you knew that you could not.

In Loving Memory

of

Georgina Louise Anderson

22nd October 1998 – 14th November 2013

Always remembered, always loved.

Georgina Anderson's song *Two Thirds of a Piece* can be downloaded at https://itunes.apple.com/gb/album/two-thirds-of-a-piece-single/id749412145

Georgina Anderson's video of her cover of Bonnie Raitt's *I Can't Make You Love Me* can be viewed at https://www.youtube.com/watch?v=BFJ8l4IVw7I

ACKNOWLEDGEMENTS

With love and thanks to my husband, Paul, and our son, Joe, for helping me to (just about) hold it together. Thanks to my mother, my sister and brother and their families, as well as to my in-laws, for the support given to us while enduring their own grief. Thanks to Chloe and Amber for being special, crazy friends to Georgina and to all of the amazing young people - especially 'Georgina's Girls' – who have been so strong for Georgina and for us. I'm sorry I can't mention you all individually.

A shout-out to the hospital and community staff – too many to name – who worked with Georgina and who continue to manage to exude compassion and positivity in a very stressful work environment. Thanks to the numerous charities involved in helping the NHS to deliver essential care to patients like Georgina and their families.

Thank you to all the celebrities and members of the public who bought Georgina's single and spread the word about her video, helping to brighten her final few days and raise vital charity funds. Thanks to Middlesbrough Football Club for going the extra mile for us.

Thank you to the friends who have supported me in completing *Piece by Piece*.

Finally, I'd like to thank all the people of Marske-by-the-Sea, the rest of the North East, and beyond, who have reached out to our family with acts of kindness and expressions of love and concern. You have helped us more than you can know.

The Teenage Cancer Trust: *Creating world-class cancer services for young people in the UK, providing life-changing care and support so young people don't have to face cancer alone.* www.teenagecancertrust.org

Clic Sargent: *Helping families deal with childhood cancer together.* www.clicsargent.org.uk

The Sick Children's Trust: *Providing free, high-quality 'Home from Home' accommodation for families with sick children in hospital.* www.sickchildrenstrust.org

Macmillan Cancer Support: *Specialist health care, information and financial support to people affected by cancer.* www.macmillan.org.uk

Rainbow Trust: *Supports families in England who have a child aged 0-18 years of age with a life threatening or terminal illness.* www.rainbowtrust.org.uk

Cancer Research UK. *Pioneering research to bring forward the day when all cancers are cured.* www.cancerresearchuk.org

Make-A-Wish UK: *Grants magical wishes to enrich the lives of children and young people fighting life-threatening conditions.* www.make-a-wish.org.uk

Coping with Cancer NE: *Shares experiences and strategies which help people cope with cancer.* www.copingwithcancer.org.uk

ABOUT THE AUTHOR

Helen Victoria Anderson was born and lives in the North-East of England. She is a prize-winning writer of poetry and prose, whose work has been published in a number of magazines and anthologies. She has an MA in Creative Writing (awarded with Distinction) from Teesside University.

To learn more about her work, visit
www.helenvictoriaanderson.co.uk

Follow Helen on Facebook at
www.facebook.com/helenvictoriaanderson

Lightning Source UK Ltd.
Milton Keynes UK
UKOW04f0502070116

265961UK00002B/20/P